Classroom Close-Ups: 6

For Art's Sake?

Classroom Close-Ups

A series edited by Gerald Haigh which tries to answer the questions 'what really happens?' and 'what really matters?' in education.

Titles published are:

1 *'Integrate!'* by Gerald Haigh
2 *Teaching Morality and Religion* by Alan Harris
3 *Early Reading and Writing: The Foundations of Literacy* by Ramin Minovi
4 *Mathematics: Friend or Foe?* by Dorothy Evans
5 *Education For Sale* by Eric Midwinter
6 *For Art's Sake?* by Jack Cross

Classroom Close-Ups: 6

Series Editor: Gerald Haigh

FOR ART'S SAKE?

A Strategic Approach to Teaching Art in Schools

Jack Cross

London
GEORGE ALLEN & UNWIN
Sydney Boston

First published in 1977

ISBN 0 04 371051 4 Hardback
0 04 371052 2 Paperback

Typeset in 10 on 11 point Press Roman
by Red Lion Setters, Holborn, London

Printed in Great Britain by
Biddles Ltd, Guildford, Surrey

Contents

For my wife Pat
whose advice I almost always take

Prologue

It says in the Old Testament that 'it is a foolish thing to make a long prologue and to be short in the story itself'. So my Prologue is short. It contains just two anecdotes, told as truthfully and objectively as I can manage; connotations, questions and conclusions will be dealt with later in the book.

The first incident took place towards the end of January 1976. A conference of heads of art departments had been convened by the county senior inspector; teachers will recognise the significance of the fact that it took place *during three days of term time* – attendance was virtually by royal command. The very first item was a seminar conducted by the inspector himself under the heading 'The Place of Art in the Secondary School Curriculum'. One of his assistants whisked through a short introduction, offering a brisk tour through the writings of the recognised authorities, quoting from Herbert Read (of course), Marion Richardson, Viktor Lowenfeldt, Elliot Eisner, *et al*., and getting more up to date by referring briefly to papers by Ernest Goodman and the new book by Robert Witkin, *The Intelligence of Feeling.* Schools Council Working Papers were held up and their reference numbers conscientiously noted down.

Meanwhile, his audience settled passively in their seats, ruminating on the iniquity of headmasters, the problems of open-plan classrooms, the possibility of wangling more equipment while they had the chance to catch the inspector off-duty and contemplating, with various degrees of equanimity, what the hell might be going on in the art rooms during their absence.

They were rudely awakened by the inspector's own very brief address, which went something like this:

'Ladies and Gentlemen, for the first time in your careers, perhaps, you are going to consider your functions in the educational world in terms of cost-effectiveness. What are you actually doing in schools and what is it worth? It is part of my job to get funds out of the Education Committee to provide you with buildings, staff and equipment and, in these times of financial retrenchment, I am increasingly being asked to justify this disbursement. I need your help. What do you do that is so valuable? How do you do it? Why do you do it that particular way. What kind of evaluation of your results would be relevant and useful?

How can I show you that the work that you do is irreplaceable?'

This was a carefully calculated piece of shock treatment from a sensitive and talented man. After it, the conference came to corporate and individual life. Art teachers who had hitherto thought of themselves as visual communicators ('I don't have to explain what I do, come into my art room and see what is on the walls') clamoured to speak. The prospect of being starved of money was, to departmental heads, the equivalent of the threat of execution. And that, as Oscar Wilde said, is 'a wonderful way to concentrate the mind'. Much of the material which appears later in this book can be attributed to the vitality of the consequent proceedings, the mixture of philosophical speculation, social analysis, pungent practical realism and intense personal involvement which my colleagues displayed in the course of three (usually eighteen-hour) days. Not for the last time this decade, I predict, was the key theme of an educational conference accountability.

My second anecdote is more personal and may contain some elements of subjectivism or even misrepresentation. If it does you will spot them and anyway I have already apologised in advance. I do happen to believe in the conclusions I have drawn and they have influenced my own curricular objectives in art and in all aspects of education ever since.

Ever since, in fact, the early 1960s when I was the landlord of a public house while continuing to teach art in a nearby town. To be honest, my wife did most of the work and I assumed the role of *patron* each evening. Externally it was not a chic establishment, indeed the guide to the region described it as looking like 'a less than prepossessing Victorian drink shop', but it was distinguished inside by a permanent but changing exhibition of modern paintings. The 'in' idiom of the time was Taschisme, or Abstract Expressionism. It was, if you remember, the kind of work it was very easy to deride. The popular press was full of stories about artists riding bicycles across their paintings and daubing their nude models with pigment before dragging and rolling them across the canvas. Most of our exhibited works were, to some degree or other, abstract in nature, tending to be derived from Pollock, Klein, Rothko or, if figurative, from the later Sutherland or Francis Bacon, who was an occasional visitor.

As you might expect, there was at first a fair amount of conventional bantering from most of the regulars, almost irrespective of class, age, occupation or previous interests, but within a very short time two contrasting attitudes emerged.

Our artisan customers – shipyard platers, welders, drillers and painters, draymen, fishermen, firemen and mechanics – began to express genuine appreciation and affection for many of the works. They would initiate discussion on the purpose and methodology of the arts and comment selectively, critically but with great open-mindedness on new paintings as they were displayed. An odd spin-off effect was that they became really expert in predicting potential saleability; their tastes coincided very closely with those of the kind of people who actually bought paintings, who had the space, inclination and cash to indulge their fancies in this way.

There were others who came especially to scoff, to hold forth about the knavish delinquency and veniality of modern artists while steadfastly keeping their backs turned towards the artefacts they were ridiculing in accents carefully maintained or cultivated in grammar or public school and in phrases which made one nostalgic for the comparative liberality of Alfred Munnings' notorious harangues at Royal Academy feasts. Even on the Essex/Suffolk border one can get very weary of hearing that there has been no great painter since (or, as far as one could tell, before) Constable. Many of the most vehement and, to my ears, insensitive statements came from people who had received higher education in what we call arts subjects, and who were mobile enough to enable them to visit most of the galleries and museums in the Western world.

I am not for a moment claiming that our working-class friends had had a superior education in art. They were, on the whole, products of the newish secondary modern schools which, outside London at any rate, were only just beginning to work out what they were for. Art as a subject had had no vocational value and tended to be dropped as pupils approached leaving-age unless it happened to be a 'soft' alternative to a more demanding subject. Few of them could claim to be able to 'draw a straight line'. But in a relaxed environment where any man's views were equally acceptable, they showed themselves (to me and the painters at least) to be pretty good judges of fairly advanced 'modern art'.

I am saying that the 'educated', middle-class people did not, in general show any superior ability in evaluating works of art unless they happened to be unique, valuable, or very old. Indeed, for reasons which may be social and psychological as well as educational, they often showed conspicuous insensitivity. I do maintain that there is little positive correlation between length of education and the development of aesthetic sensibility. Surely, in a civilised society, there should be?

Why, you may well be asking, choose this particular piece of uncharacteristic experience to support a general thesis about the function of art in the curriculum? Primarily because it is about adults. Education is not, strictly speaking, for children; it is for potential men and women, husbands and fathers, wives and mothers, employees and bosses, buyers and sellers, entertainers and audience.

J. D. Bruner writes 'We might ask, as a criterion for any subject taught in a school, whether, fully developed, it is worth an adult's knowing and whether having known it as a child makes a person a better adult. If the answer to both questions is negative or ambiguous then the material is cluttering up the curriculum' (*The Process of Education*, 1960).

There are many ways of identifying and describing educational objectives. Art specialists are no different from most of their colleagues in being too busy, too involved, too set in their ways perhaps, to ask themselves the primary questions very often. A pragmatic posture often appears the most appropriate. But most of us have felt threatened in recent years by the apparent rejection by large numbers of our pupils of the values and systems we have taken for granted all our lives. The questions are now, perforce, being asked. We may feel that the greatest pressures come from within the school system – comprehensive reorganisation, ROSLA, and so on. Others sense that the motive force for change comes from outside, from shifts and cracks in the social structure itself. As Marshall McLuhan wrote (in a kind of *vers libre*):

> Today in our cities
> Most learning occurs outside the classroom.
> The sheer quantity of information conveyed by
> The press-mags, films, TV., radio
> far exceeds
> The quantity of information conveyed by
> school instruction and texts.
> This challenge has destroyed
> The monopoly of the book as a teaching aid
> and cracked the very walls of the classroom
> so suddenly,
> we're confused, baffled.[1]

Now it is obviously true that many teachers do not feel baffled at all, or, if they do, they do not allow it to show. What was good enough for 4C last year will be fine for the renamed 4BC2(f) this, and if they do not get their GCEs, whose fault is that? But discussion about curricular priorities is in the air, which accounts for the proliferation of faculty and interdepartmental discussion groups and the appointment of directors of study in the larger schools. Teachers are finding it increasingly necessary to justify their positions, something they have not had to do for many years. Art teachers are frequently in the vanguard of the questioning brigade. Perhaps it is because of the traditional lowly status of their subject, perhaps because they have

[1] From G. E. Stearns (ed.), *McLuhan Hot and Cool* (Penguin, 1968).

wider parameters of choice; maybe their chosen vocation has given them more sensitive antennae to tune them in to the changing world. At any rate they have evolved, individually and in groups, more rationales, more teaching strategies, a wider range of identifiable objectives, than those of any other subject I can think of. It will be my task in this book to classify the aims and methods of a variety of teachers and to examine them in the light of the twin needs of our pupils: the *immediate*, while the child is still in school, and the *future*, when he enters fully into the life of the community.

Art rooms are normally untidy places with ephemera-filled walls and busy, cluttered surfaces, but they always embody, whether consciously or not, some kind of curricular strategy. I owe my thanks to those of my colleagues who have allowed themselves to be inveigled into discarding the usual visual artist's defence of avoiding verbalising and have accepted that, just for once, the word can be as useful as the brush.

PART I: THE SUBJECT

Chapter 1

What Is Art?

It is perhaps a trifle unusual to begin a book about a recognised school subject by asking what that subject is all about. Still, better at the beginning than the end, like that old but standard little work which finishes something like this: 'What it intelligence? We have had to assume that intelligence is that which is measured by intelligence tests.' You may take it that I will not offer a definition which suggests that art is that which satisfies the CSE, O or A-level examiners. But it is, I maintain, an important question and whatever his answer to it may be, it should, and does, affect the whole range of the teacher's objectives and activities in the art room.

Conventionally it is only the 'new' subject areas which need to be defined. Broadly speaking, everybody knows what to expect from a course in history (about chaps), geography (maps), and Latin; it is only when they are transmuted into social, environmental, European or classical studies that their parameters and priorities need to be defined. In the traditional subjects there may be certain choices and disagreements, but these are largely about emphasis. A geography teacher, for example, who gives a lot of his time to interdisciplinary local study may be criticised as being a shade parochial in his approach, but is it unlikely that he will be told that what he is doing is 'not geography'.

It is a different matter for the artist – or the teacher of art. Every man and his brother feels perfectly entitled to say of a French Impressionist painting, a Picasso drawing, an Epstein sculpture, a pile of bricks in the Tate Gallery or a giant model of a cigarette butt that 'it's not art'. Of course he may well be right, which stimulates the critic to draw in his perimeter of acceptance even more tightly to the point where it positively excludes anything which is strange, antagonistic or challenging to his own pre-set notions. Art teachers themselves are not immune to aesthetic dogma. Brian Allison, Principal of Leicester College of Art, once proposed a law which stated that the range of art products which people in general prefer and profess to understand is bounded precisely by the limits of the kind of art with which their teachers were familiar when they completed their training.

No definition of art can be completely satisfying or beyond dispute. The dictionary is not really very helpful, it leaves too much out.

'**Art**, n. Skill, esp. human skill as opposed to nature;
skilful execution as an object in itself;
skill applied to imitation & design, as in painting, etc.'

(*Concise Oxford*, 1964)

But it does point to one factor which ought to be a cliché but is not. It emphasises that art is about human skill. *In art the process is more important than the product.* This is something for the art teacher to ponder about because it runs counter to his experience of 'real art' in the outside world. In a modern consumer society art is a product, a marketable *thing*, the value of which is determined by factors like recognisable originality, rarity and uniqueness or, as in the world of popular prints, by ubiquity and familiarity. The teacher is in intimate contact with pupils who are engaged in making art, with whatever degree of success, and it is they who are his real concern rather than the works which they may produce. It may be necessary for him to argue this point (with his head teacher who expects a continuous supply of recognisably 'good' art to impress the parents and governors, or with his colleagues who believe that everything pinned up in the art room should, necessarily, be 'the best'.

How can one identify the essential ingredients of genuine art – producing activity? Maurice Barratt and Robert Witkin have divided it into three components whose interdependence is demonstrated in Figure 1. There are, they say, three elements of creative activity which they call Conceptual, Operational and Synthetic; all must be present, working upon each other and in balance, to produce an authentic piece of art:

(i) *Conceptual* – having ideas, thinking, feeling, forming concepts, responding to experience, remembering, observing, etc.;

(ii) *Operational* – using tools, choosing and using materials, developing appropriate skills, etc.;

(iii) *Synthetic* – putting it all together, using a form which can best express the concept through the use of the medium.

You will have noted that the diagram is circular; the circle is the ancient symbol for a never-finishing, continually inter-reactive process. As Eric Newton wrote:

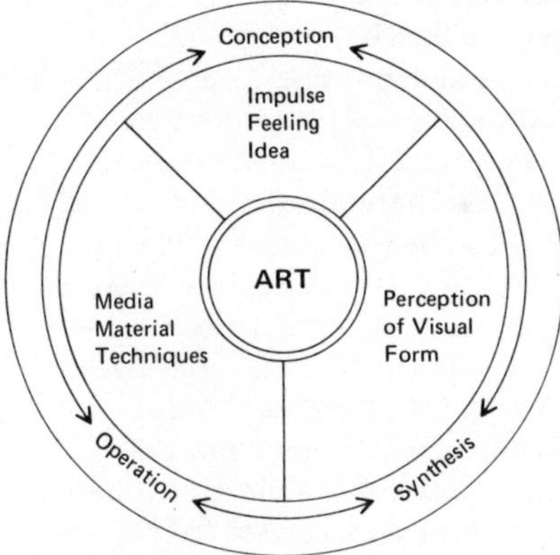

Figure 1

'Every artist knows from experience, but few laymen ever realise, the constant interplay between mind and hand as a work of art progresses. The layman might suppose that all the artist has to do is to call up in the imagination an image, as complete as he can make it, of the work he intends to produce and then translate it into his chosen or prescribed medium. But that is by no means an accurate account of the creative process. The original, imagined image is actually far from complete, and as soon as the artist sets to work his medium begins to modify and clarify it; unless he is a bad artist, he will accept and take advantage of these modifications.'[1]

'This is all very well', I can hear a teacher-critic say, 'for real artists. We are concerned with children, beginners; surely we should make it easier for them, separate the strands, isolate the appropriate skills and *teach* them. They may put it all together, later.' I am afraid this just is not so. Fifth-form Sally, working away at her clay model, is behaving like an artist much more than she is as an historian, scientist or mathematician in her other studies. She is thinking, feeling, manipulating, putting together, and her original concept is changing under her hands.

What happens when we, as teachers, separate the creative components, divide the indivisible? It depends, of course, which of the elements we tend to over-emphasise – usually the one we happen to teach best.

The self-expression movement was and is the product of too much concentration on the *conceptual* element. A liberating force in earlier

[1] *The Meaning of Beauty* (Pelican, 1952).

years it has, in the words of one art teacher, engendered the 'curse of creativity', encouraged a do-your-own-thing mentality which has produced a lot of 'self-indulgent slop'. Very hard words, but it can hardly be denied that in a lot of art rooms you will find displayed works which, though superficially bright and exciting, seem very immature. After a certain maturation age (very, very approximately about the age of 9) it can be frustrating rather than liberating for a child to have a strong and personal impulse to communicate and find that he lacks the technical skill, experience of alternative media or sense of form to convey it satisfactorily. Have you, like me, visited exhibitions of children's art where work is arranged without relation to age and, having responded with enjoyment to a particular work, found that what you had experienced as a piece of colourful, direct expression admirable in a primary school child was, in fact, the product of an older pupil – and immediately felt let down? It can be very dangerous to fall in love with 'child art' unless you adore Peter Pan.

It is equally, perhaps more, common for teachers to try to teach techniques for their own sake, stressing the *operational* functions early in the belief that they will be of use later on. It is probably the most respectable of the separatist doctrines as it is, in every sense of the word, truly 'academic'. Classes practise rote exercises in the use of tools and implements, paint colour wheels, copy the teacher's drawings to learn ever more sophisticated developments of linear perspective, practise the use of tone, and so on. For some teachers, very few now I hope, the important thing is to get it right. I can remember a teaching practise where the student, while presiding over a gloriously free co-operative effort to produce an abstract mural, received a daunting visit from the headmaster. He dismayed her by grunting, as he left the room, that he preferred it when he had not got an art teacher. Then he took the subject himself. 'I put up a bucket, give every boy a 2B pencil and tell him to draw it. I go round with a red pen and cross off the lines they get wrong. I don't allow rubbers; if they get it really wrong I make them do it again!'

It is probably true that the search for an appropriate form to express an idea is the most difficult task the artist-pupil has to face. It is very tempting to help him by teaching certain set forms to him direct. So we find art teachers sketching a skeletal landscape or figure composition on the blackboard and inviting the class to fill it from their own imagination. Such crutches are even more common in pottery and the other crafts where there are so many helpful books of 'Creative this, that or the other' to give the children a leg up. This must account for the number of times and the variety of places in which that cylindrical coiled-clay cat and pinch-pot piggybank appear.

I hereby confess that I have been guilty, from time to time, of most of the deviations and distortions caricatured above though I do not think I have ever asked a class to draw a bucket with 2B pencils. In fact no one need feel guilty for occasionally, even regularly, applying his teaching to one or other of the separate art-producing functions. It is clearly an economical use of teaching time if some of it is given to showing and discussing stimulating images, some to training the pupils in skills for which the majority have shown a clear need, and some in pointing out – perhaps with the aid of slides, strips and film – how difficult formal problems have been solved by adult artists. But it is important to remember that only when fusion has taken place, when the pupils are working on their own, is genuine art activity taking place. Art teachers are only supervising creativity part of the time.

It will have been noticed that this book has been and will continue to be concerned with the visual arts. Much of what has been written in this chapter applies equally well to, say, writing a poem, creating a drama, making a film. All the muses command the same kind of service. But, in common parlance, there is a clear distinction between the arts and art, which is usually recognised in the organisation of schools. Painting, pottery, printing, etc. are art; they take place in the art department. Drama belongs to the empire of the English master. Music is a separate subject handled by its own specialists, combining only with the other arts when they are wanted to reinforce a special production or occasion. Dance belongs to the gymnasium; it is part, sometimes an odd part, of physical education. Often one finds informal combinations of teachers crossing the boundaries; some of the more usual interdisciplinary organisations are discussed later in Chapter 10. Generally speaking, however, art in this book is taken to mean the activities which take place in the art room.

Many art teachers live and work in unenviable freedom within the school community. They are expected to dress, think and behave rather differently from their colleagues who often do not profess to understand or care very much about what they are actually trying to do. They are sometimes taken to task for not developing in their pupils skills which would be useful in other areas: 'I took 2A out on environmental studies and not one of them could draw the castle in perspective!' Apart from blinding the complainant with science by talking about the appropriate developmental and maturational level at which such arcane mysteries should be introduced, the art teacher can best defend himself by upholding the inherent identity of art as a subject in itself. It is not an adjunct to something else. It is concerned with making and doing, not with what has been made. It is about emotion, expression, sensibility and conceptualisation. It cares about offering each individual a chance to communicate his own feeling in his own chosen way. It is about individual needs and personal judgements. Freedom through discipline is its object – is it not of all education?

Chapter 2

What Is an Artistically Educated Person?

5A have got their heads down. They entered the art room quietly, collected their uncompleted work in an orderly way they would not have dreamed of last term and most of them are already drawing away, with the exception of a couple of girls in the corner who have found the copies of *Valentine* which they are using to support their papers a bit too distracting – they are discussing the implications of their horoscopes. What motivates this unusual conscientiousness? A casual glance at the work in progress should offer a clue. One group is carefully drawing a disembowelled pencil-sharpener, another producing shaded sketches of a lump of coal. Quite a lot of them, mostly girls, are practising calligraphy, using their own vigilantly guarded pens to copy out lines of poetry which have been chosen, more or less at random, from one of the anthologies in the bookshelf. There is a lot of lettering of all kinds, its practitioners glancing from time to time at tattered foolscap sheets of typescript which they have taken from their folders. There is a muttered curse as one boy points out to his mate a spelling error in the latter's poster for a school production of *Romeo and Juliet* (which has not and will not take place).

Of course, it is the beginning of the spring term; GCE mocks are imminent and everybody knows that well-prepared mock papers are the foundation of the course-work folder for Paper 6 (for this is a school which traditionally takes the Cambridge examinations).

Unfortunately, as the teacher reminds them, they are not supposed to be doing practical work at all – this is a theory lesson and only he knows the arguments and politicking which were necessary to get it on to the timetable at all. Normally it is a period which he enjoys most, when he can put aside his instructor's role and don the imaginary toga of a pseudo-Socrates. This is a bright lot, the ex-grammar stream, you can talk to them about things that matter without having to simplify so much as to make the exercise meaningless.

Proceed always from the known to the unknown. 'Come on now,

pay a bit of attention, you need not stop drawing altogether if you are as keen as all that. But tell me – what are you doing?'

'Drawing this bit of broken bone, Sir.'

'Why? Do you particularly like it as an object? What do you find interesting about it?'

'It's got a lot of texture in the broken bit.'

'Good, is that why you chose it?'

'Yes Sir, they're very keen on textures in the Objective Drawing Paper, you've always said.'

Pause. Start again. 'OK, you're doing something called objective drawing. What does "objective" mean?'

Chris, whose student brother occasionally brings home copies of *Time Out*, mutters something about 'tell it like it is man', and, with relieving chuckles all round, O-level prescriptions temporarily forgotten, the discussion begins to gather some momentum.

'Sir, what do you think of modern art?'

This is an important question, not to be dodged. It is, perhaps, one of the oddities of teaching that one deals with pupils who consign a pop record to the dustbin of forgetfulness after it has been out of the charts for more than a week, yet cheerfully consider the works of men who would be old enough to be their great-grandfathers if they still lived to be either childish or dangerously subversive. This does not necessarily proceed from insensitivity; nor is it an unjust impeachment. Any student who has gained some status in the school community by what he knows, remembers and can explain, and who intends to get more by the same techniques, may well feel threatened when faced by the challenge of the unknown, unexplained and apparently inexplicable. The printed page, principal tool of education, is, in McLuhan's terminology, a 'cold' medium – so, on the whole, is school. With the best will in the world our system seems to embody the idea that 'intelligence and feeling can be separated and that the development of the former is by far the most important and should be the dominating preoccupation of schools'.[1] It is largely the constraints of our socio-educational system which have contributed to what T. S. Eliot called the 'disassociation of the sensibility' – and probably for the existence of the art-blind but otherwise apparently educated, far-from-silent majority I encountered in my public-house exhibitions.

If it is to be my task in the later chapters of this book to lay out for inspection the various strategies which may be deployed to increase the numbers of 'artistically educated persons' it is, perhaps, necessary at this stage to describe what such a paragon would be like. What kind of

[1] Ernest Goodman, *Curriculum Justification*. (The collected papers of the Association of Art Advisers.)

personality, in the long term, is all our art education intended to produce?

Such a person must believe that art is an important element in his life and in the continuing life of his community. He should know, feel, accept, that the aesthetic response is as valid an attitude to experience as the other modes fostered in his education – mathematical, historical, scientific or whatever. This is hardly the 'normal' position given to the arts in our contemporary society, in which art may be thought of as:

(i) a respectable and relaxing hobby;
(ii) a rather superior kind of interior decoration;
(iii) an opportunity for eccentric self-expression;
(iv) an excuse for adopting a freer life style;
(v) or the prestigious product of a special kind of person (the genius) for the delectation and admiration of the rest of us. It was one of the less happy results of the European Renaissance that it tended to sever the lines of communication between the makers and observers of art objects.

Imagine a lesson in which the teacher tries to convey some sense of the *necessity of art* to other forms of society. He will, quite possibly, start with cave paintings of the Upper Paleolithic Age. 'Think', he will say, 'of a life in which almost everything is inimical to man. The animals are all faster, bigger, better-armed, better clad – yet he must live off them or die. The total resources of the tribe, the labour of every man, woman and child is dedicated to the act of preserving its existence – hunting animals, tending the fire, preserving food through the long cold winters, making clothes. Passengers are an impossible luxury, the elderly and incapable must be allowed to perish in the interest of the survival of the group. Everyone must work and earn his keep. Yet, as we know (and here those awesome images of Altamira appear on the screen) many people, for generation after generation, were employed in scratching lines and daubing pigments on the walls of fire-lit caves. Almost certainly they were men – because of the evidence of intimate knowledge of the hunt; maybe some of them were lamed or otherwise incapable of foraging with the rest – but they were allowed to live and, as far as we can tell, were given honourable status in the group. Why should this be so? What did they do that was so important?'

It is probably being over-optimistic to expect a group of twentieth-century adolescents to educe intuitively the concept of the artist/shaman/priest who used magically compulsive images to aid in the psychic preparation of pathetically armed hunters. Even so the teacher is likely to be deflated by the stock responses he will get to his prepared question: 'Why were these paintings/painters important to the community?' 'As decorations; they passed the time; it was something to do – they were done for fun.'

Where then to start? I know of no better way than the shock treatment proposed by Professor Gombrich: 'Suppose we take a picture of our favourite cricketer or film star (in contemporary terms pop-star, footballer or boy friend): would we enjoy taking a needle and poking out its eyes? Would we feel as indifferent about it as if we poked the hole elsewhere on the paper?'[1] It may seem odd to have to call upon ancient folk memories of the practices of witchcraft to make a pedagogic breakthrough but it does often work.

Another element necessary for aesthetic appreciation is, I suggest, the ability to see a work of art for what it is and not as an expression of something else – a political or social message, a precise record of natural phenomena or artefact (but one slightly inferior to a photograph), a token of delight in an attractive sitter or an enjoyed landscape – but as an *object* which has been imagined, conceived, pondered over, worked on and made. It will be my contention that all the usual activities of the art room, all the drawing, painting, potting and printing, find their true purpose not so much in the gratification of the makers as in the fostering of a kind of understanding of the nature of all created work.

It is important for the artistically educated person to be able to distinguish clearly between the purposes and qualities of art and craft. A craftsman visualises the perfect result in advance and all his further activities are directed towards the achievement of the original idea. There is usually a nice separation of functions – thinking, sketching, making working drawings, using tools – which works well to the teacher's advantage.

But the artist cannot, must not, know in advance exactly how his work will end. The demands of the medium, his own responses to it, the actual developing existence of the work in progress, all operate to modify his evolving conception.

One must be prepared for accidental discoveries: 'Art loves chance and chance loves art.' So it becomes the art teacher's duty to send out individual pupils on voyages with no foreseeable conclusions. It can be a daunting and confidence-sapping experience for them and a perpetual challenge to him. The very existence of so many well-illustrated books and magazines devoted to specialised crafts seems to produce a sameness in the work of schools where the two-dimensional work is often much more individual and expressive.

One contemporary trap awaits the potential art evaluator: it might be called pseudo-democracy – 'It's a free country, isn't it? I've as much

[1] Ernst H. Gombrich, *The History of Art* (Phaidon, 1972).

right to my opinion as anyone else!' It is part of the teacher's job to isolate those elements of criticism which may be objectivised; to tread the narrow path between 'this is good because history and I say it is and you'd better believe it' and 'this is splendid because you enjoyed doing it'. Perhaps the most observable and teachable standards are those which concern the internal consistency of a work. As Wittgenstein says, 'Art is a game where rules are made up as the game is in progress, where the exact meaning of words or images is known only in the context of each new statement or articulation' (*Philosophical Investigations*). The 'rules of the game' concept is a very useful one to use; pupils know very well that if you pick up the ball you have either ruined a good game of soccer – or invented rugby.

I see that I have very much emphasised the cognitive elements in art teaching and make no apology for doing so. It is the strategies of thinking, ways of looking, seeing, analysing, recording, evaluating, that will be needed in later life, rather than the abilities to handle pencil, brush, squeegee and template. Art education inevitably contains a great deal of making and doing but, I maintain, this is largely because such activities provide unique insights into the nature of art by introducing the child to the intimate experience of the choices and tactics open to the artist at work.

Finally, it must always be remembered that art is the expression and communication of feeling. Distilled and disciplined though it must be, it has to spring from an intensely personal, physical response to the natural world. It is very easy to trample on personal feelings in the classroom; in a subject where value judgements are important the danger is always present. Older pupils, in particular, quiver and sway in the gusts of succeeding fashions. One sensational TV programme about Andy Warhol, one set of Turner postage stamps, and the teacher is faced with a host of immature and superficial imitations. Horror comics provide a never ending series of banal but powerful images which the kids love to reproduce. Even these can be discussed, refined, redeployed to provide genuine metaphors for adolescent fantasy. It does not do for the teacher to indulge too much his own aesthetic snobbery. To build in constraints and limitations is no part of the conscientious teacher's brief. Unfortunately the more intelligent and highly motivated the pupil the more easily does he absorb the teacher's standards. After all the rest of the curriculum seems like that. Mr Smith demonstrates Pythagoras, and it works. One authoritative textbook will see him through his history exams. Art is a school subject – does it not work that way too?

But 5A is made of sterner stuff and spokesman Chris has more than one shot in his locker so he produces a block-buster. 'Sir', he says, with mock humility, 'how do you know when a painting is any good?' Would anyone care to answer?

Chapter 3

How Art Got into the Curriculum and What Happened when It Arrived

This book is supposed to be about current trends in education. At first sight, therefore, a dissertation on the historical antecedents of art teaching might seem rather out of place. I do not believe this to be true. The British tradition, in education as in much else, depends a great deal on the concept of continuity, on precedent broadening into precedent. Although in any one teacher's working life changes may appear to come in giant steps (back or forward, according to opinion) such developments, when they are concerned with the curriculum and teaching methods, are rarely very drastic. It is a different matter, of course, when it comes to the administrative structure of the educational system and the organisation of schools themselves. But this country still maintains a system in which the head is allowed a great deal of autonomy as to what is taught in his school. Subject teachers may not possess the same freedom, though art specialists are often exceptions to this rule, if only because their subject is not always understood and is frequently underestimated. The art teacher, therefore, is able to choose his objectives, methods and style from a menu which is as long as the history of the subject itself. The headmaster mentioned in Chapter 1, for instance, he of the bucket and hard pencil, would have been perfectly at home preparing his pupils for the Second-Grade Model-Drawing Test set by the Department of Science and Art in 1870 (Figure 2).

One clear inheritance from the past is the persistent official desire to justify art (or, as it was always called in the early days, drawing) as a 'useful subject'; what Herbert Read has called the 'art as adjunct' concept. This was not too difficult to do in the early nineteenth century in schools which were designed for the sons of the middle classes. Would it not be nice for them to be able to record their

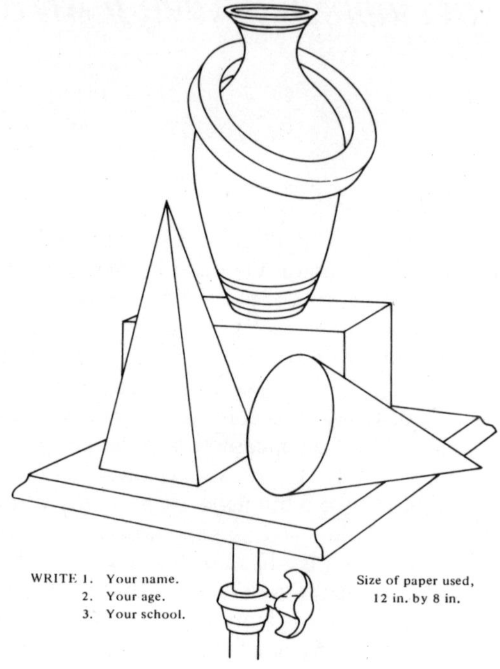

Fig. 2

impressions of the customary foreign travels in line and wash? A young gentleman who could draw could use his skill to supplement his diary; the school provided the services of a drawing master as an optional extra, for an additional fee. During the century not only was there an expansion of educational provision for the children of the artisan class, but drawing lessons were also introduced in the schools for the poor. The reason was strictly utilitarian. British goods were unsuccessfully competing with their continental equivalents because their level of design was poor. Much home-produced work was, in fact, based on pirated European designs and patterns. Manufacturers pressed for the encouragement of native talent. In 1835 a House of Commons Select Committee considered 'The Best Means of Extending a Knowledge of

Art and the Principles of Design among the People (especially the Manufacturing Population of the Country'. Its deliberations led to the establishment of the Somerset House School of Design and, soon afterwards, to other schools in the provinces. A start had been made – for sound commercial reasons. Teachers were offered drawing courses in the 'normal schools' and colleges and given welcome additions to their stipends if they were successful. Step by step, the teaching of drawing entered the elementary schools.

What the children learnt was not, in any sense of the term, fine art. The post-Freudian notion of child art was as yet inconceivable. There was a great deal of copying from flat outlines, usually on slates, from drawings themselves copied onto the blackboard by teachers using compulsory set books containing plates of prepared examples. These shapes were simple (they had to be, they were to be 'corrected' by monitors), geometrical (although the books contained illustrations which were obviously produced with the use of instruments, such aids were strictly forbidden for use by the child), and very formal. 'This is how you should draw a fish, bird, bell, vase, iris, etc.' There was a certain amount of lettering practice, both of calligraphic penmanship and of approved decorative capitals. In fact 'ornament', a very specific, highly derivative and rigidly conventional discipline, was considered very important, in itself a justification for teaching drawing. After all, it could be of value to industry: 'The interests of commerce are so intimately connected with the results to be obtained by this branch of elementary education that there is little chance that it will much longer suffer the grievous neglect which it has hitherto experienced' (*Report to the Poor Law Commissioners*, 1841). Incidentally, if anyone believes that this intense dedication to the cause of the industrial exploitation of art died with the century I can simply record that I visited a Middlesex school as late as 1965 and was told that it pursued exclusively utilitarian objectives in *all* subjects. Craft was metalwork and engineering, Science was metallurgy, the English was of the commercial variety, and so on. Art was lettering, poster design, packaging and publicity. The school's avowed aim was to prepare its students for careers in the many light engineering factories which surrounded its site.

But to return to the nineteenth century and Victorian educational ideology; it is tempting to oversimplify the way in which every activity, including art, could be squeezed into the mould. Drawing was practical and could be put to commercial use in a way which was overtly patriotic. It was also moral and encouraged industrious habits. Training in accurate observation could make children 'all the more truthful and sensible of God's wisdom'. Classroom pictures offered for study and emulation – usually illustrations of biblical texts – were spiritually elevating. There has always been a rather touching, though totally unproven, educational belief in art as a moral force in society. This belief is reflected in a passage from the Norwood Report of 1941, which urged that 'there may be kept before children the importance of Art as a powerful influence for good or ill in modern life, the enrichment which it can bring to their lives and their own responsibility as its guardians in the future'. The 'art as adjunct' thesis again – expressed in social and spiritual terms.

Within the apparently rigid and stable Victorian society dynamic forces were at work. After Darwin, Marx and Freud the world could never be quite the same again. Official attitudes were being challenged, not least in the field of education. Art teaching was not exempt, indeed new perceptions about the nature of childhood gave it an additional importance. Many eminent people began to take an interest in the notion of children's art work as a valuable activity in its own right. Herbert Spencer, the philosopher, was one of the first writers to insist that art was a *process*, important to individual development: 'The question is not whether the child is producing good drawings. The question is, whether it is developing its faculties.'[1]

This is not the place to list the contributions of such people as Ruskin, Froebal, Dyce, William Morris and Ebenezer Cooke to the enlightenment of art educators during the second half of the nineteenth century. Gordon Sutton's recent book, *Artisan or Artist?*, traces their influence step by step in precise and intriguing detail. What they were saying, each in his own way, was that the 'liberalisation' of the curriculum, which was generally considered desirable, depended upon drastic modifications in teaching methods. It would not suffice to offer the pupils some choice of what they should draw and the opportunity to colour it or not. In effect, they maintained (in the language used in Chapter 1 of this book) that the *operational* function of drawing had been grotesquely overstressed.

The publication, in 1905, of the Board of Education's *Suggestions to Teachers* registers the impact of the reformers. Almost for the first time art teachers were required to consider the real needs of individual children of different ages and at different stages of development. They were to try to make drawing a pleasant and popular activity, to encourage larger, freer work, to look for the expression of imagination and creativity. Art teachers were to be less concerned with training and more with psychological insight and artistic values.

Change did not come overnight; in many schools it did not come at all. There were still many proponents of positive skill training: 'You cannot expect originality from children, teach them to do things right!'

[1] 'On Education – What Knowledge Is Most Worth?' in *Essays on Education* (Dent, 1911, 1949).

The flat copying of conventionally outlined shapes continued (I was taught this way myself in my junior school in the 1930s). The use of orthodox ornamental motifs went on. But it was by now recognised that the design of an art curriculum depended on the resolution of the problem of reconciling three basic forces:

(i) the nature of the child (psychology);
(ii) the nature of art (aesthetic theory);
(iii) the institution (national policy, organisation of schools, training of teachers, provision of equipment and material, etc.).

This is just as true today.

What had not changed was the persistent desire to *justify* the existence of art in the curriculum in terms outside its own. The Hadow Report of 1926 stated that:

'In no other subject has there been in the last half century a greater advance in the methods of teaching than in those of Drawing and Art. The greater respect now given to the subject is due in part to the improved methods of teaching and in part to a realisation of its value in the teaching of other subjects. A further reason is a greater recognition of the importance to the whole community of a finer taste, not only or even chiefly in pictures and sculpture, but in architecture, in furniture, in household crafts. In the formation of such taste drawing must be one of the chief means'.

Passing quickly over what the Committee call the 'artistic side' with the comment that 'the lines along which this development should take place are well established and well understood', they then deal in much more detail with the utilitarian value of art training.

'. . . some practical skill in drawing forms a valuable and indeed an indispensable adjunct to the study of various branches of the curriculum such as woodwork and metalwork, elementary geometry, elementary science, particularly nature study, biology and mechanics, geography and history . . . to appreciate the significance of diagrams, pictures, maps and plans in the textbooks and works of reference . . .'.

This well-known document nowhere defines the well-established and well-understood lines of development to which it refers. The Committee probably meant the ideas of the New Art movement which had sprung up and was getting a great deal of publicity, gathering disciples among art teachers in the period between the wars. This was not a unified body, possessed no single dogma, issued no authoritative manifesto: it represented a body of opinion, intuitively felt, about the purposes and principles which art education should serve. Stimulated by the research and writings of psychologists like Stanley Hall, Cyril Burt and Herbert Read, translated into devoted practice by committed teachers like Marion Richardson, supported by members of the inspectorate, notably London's R. R. Tomlinson, it seemed to offer a new vision of the role of the teacher of the arts. Whatever the general practice in other subjects, he should be different – more passive, an assistant rather than a guide, a follower of natural development rather than the imprinter of adult concepts, a sort of aesthetic and spiritual midwife. For better or worse, this 'different' image remains. 'If arts teachers are felt to be in important respects a group apart, the individual arts teacher often suffers from a considerable degree of professional isolation' (*Arts and the Adolescent*, Schools Council Working Paper no. 54, 1975).

The New Art movement was, generally speaking, victorious: its ideas were accepted, taught to trainee teachers, practised in the schools. Yet this very triumph had two faces. While it is inspiring to see how an unorganised band of scattered enthusiasts could create a reform movement which could radically change the concepts of a profession, all innovators should take warning from what happened later. It is salutary to observe how each new idea could so easily become distorted, lose its freshness and degenerate into a stale (if comparatively new) academism.

It cannot be denied that Herbert Read shed a great deal of light on the true nature of the young artist's imagination and gave an intellectual substructure to the subject which enormously improved its status in the schools. But his psychological theories were grossly overdeployed, exaggerated often to the point of idiocy. His followers made a fetish of studying individual pieces of art work for hidden revelations of inherent personality traits and subconscious stress. Read himself was not immune. I have before me his seminal *Education through Art* open at two illustrations on facing pages. About one of these, 'The Witches', the author comments that 'The expressionist element tends to predominate over the imaginative. Probably introverted sensation type.' The other picture shows a girl looking out of a window. Read notes that 'Haptic expression is shown in the over-emphasised head and the under-sized cat.' Happily very few art teachers indulge themselves in this kind of instant analysis today, though it was quite common in the 1940s and 1950s.

Marion Richardson's followers, too, tended to do her ideas a disservice by slavish imitation. It is true that she did encourage children to work on a grand scale if they wanted to, that almost single-handed she introduced powder paint into the art room to replace those once universal, hard-cake water-colour boxes, that her pupils produced abstract 'thought-pictures' and memory drawings rather than copies from life, but in the wrong hands her methods produced crude caricatures which were, rightly, damned by critics as the 'art of slosh'. The pattern work associated with writing, to which she gave her name, pervaded the art rooms of the country, producing the very dull, imperceptive, sameness of scene which she most hated.

If this sameness is less evident today this is more likely to be due to the introduction of crafts into the art departments than to any radical change in the philosophy and methods of teaching painting and drawing; these are no longer the sole, or even main, preoccupations of a large body of modern teachers of art. It has been argued that about the age of puberty crafts should take over from child art and lead the pupil into the purposeful seriousness of more mature expression. In the modern primary school art and craft are almost interchangeable terms. One has only to study a catalogue of any of the firms specialising in educational art equipment and material to realise the vast variety available and in general use in schools. Certainly any gathering of art teachers will produce a much more lively discussion about new equipment (or possible ways of improvising alternatives for it) than it will about curricular objectives or methodology. Having traced the process by which drawing became art, how, these teachers may well ask, did art become art and craft?

Midway through the nineteenth century, a subject appeared on many timetables variously labelled as manual training, hand and eye training, handwork, handicraft or applied art. What varied and was argued over for the best part of a century was the appropriate balance between the art (or expressive) component and skill training. The argument still goes on, both in contemporary conglomerates in which art and the traditional crafts are supposed to merge and within art departments themselves.

The dichotomy was, and is, less pronounced at the lower end of the age range. No one really every believed that 6- to 7-year-olds could begin to learn a trade. There was quite a lot of fairly free elementary craftwork in Victorian kindergarten and infant schools. Activities like modelling in clay or plasticine, wool embroidery on coarse canvas (samplers, for example), knitting, plaiting in paper leading on to simple weaving, paper and card constructions, were encouraged as 'natural' and educationally valuable. But then it was all dropped until the child reached the age of 12 when, if he were a boy, he might be allowed to spend a couple of hours a week in a workshop. This would be a separate manual training centre, staffed by a craftsman rather than a teacher – there are records of caretakers and janitors taking short courses of instruction in order to staff such centres for extra pay. For the girls there was, of course, needlework. But it is clear that for both, if a systematic course in handwork were offered, it would be a dull repetitive process devoted to the acquisition of useful skills.

It was the search for a curriculum suitable for the middle years of schooling, between the ages of, say, 8 and 11, that provided the battleground for the struggle between those who favoured the pre-eminence of the disciplinary values of craftsmanship against those who stressed the expressive values of art. In spite of William Morris and the Pre-Raphaelites, Renaissance man was dead. Two historical concepts were opposed. The craftsman tended to think of art as a decoration of life rather than central to it. Others considered craft to be purely vocational, without intellectual or aesthetic merit. These attitudes combined only in keeping both disciplines apart and preventing them from contributing to the mainstream of education. The New Art movement, with its emphasis on free expression, only served to increase the gulf.

All the major educational reports of the twentieth century have stressed the importance of reconciling these differences in attitude. They have not entirely succeeded. Most craft teachers can produce their stereotype of the art teacher who encourages his pupils to mount their tiles on a crude frame knocked together with butt-joint, panel pins, glue and blind faith. The artist conceives of craft training to be so concerned with the perfection of tool using and joint making that very little gets made – and that rarely original. In fact these caricatures are now by no means universally applicable. In general, the disciplines have remained separate but the practitioners have absorbed each other's values, though applying them, fairly strictly, to their own areas of study. So we have art teachers who are excellent craft printers, enamellers and potters. (Pottery is particularly interesting: there was a period in which it was not uncommon to find this subject alone in no-man's-land, responsible to neither side.) At the same time craft teachers have tried to throw off the shackles of their individual specialisations and to become more concerned with the design element of their subject. It is perhaps not for me, an art teacher, to comment too authoritatively on their comparative failure, the traditions of their trade and the vocational bias of their pupils have frequently been too strong for them.

In modern comprehensives it is not uncommon for the officially desired end to be sought through organisation, grouping together teachers of art and the various crafts in new units called design centres or art/craft faculties. In individual circumstances these may work, but very often they find that they have merely provided quite lavish accommodation for some very mixed and uncomfortable bedfellows.

Perhaps the most fruitful attempt to reconcile the two cultures is to be found in the courses which were developed in the technical colleges of Leeds, Durham and Leicester about the mid-1960s, going under the general heading of 'visual education' or 'basic design'. Such curricula aim to relate, in educational terms, the social, economic, technical and aesthetic aspects of contemporary life and to study them in terms of a totally integrated union of art and craft (see chapter 9).

Let me make a final apology for this historical sketch. Almost every kind of teaching process which has been employed in the past can be observed every day in our schools. Every art teacher was taught by someone who was, in his turn, influenced by *his* teachers. The most modern curricular strategy was not immaculately conceived. There is no common body of knowledge and intention to offer guidance to the art teacher and, if there were, there is no authority willing to impose it. We pick and choose and our models come from the past. There has been development, of course, but the earlier strands can still be distinguished. The contemporary equivalents of and evolutions from the movements outlined in this chapter are more closely examined in Chapters 4 to 9.

PART II: THE POSSIBILITIES

Chapter 4

A Choice of Objectives

The following advice to parents on how to assess a school, recently appeared in the *Guardian:*

'If you can find out who is responsible for the school's curriculum, then try to get an explanation as to why teachers teach what they do that goes back beyond the surface assertions of intellectual fashion to a thought – a philosophy. As a test case, the art teacher might be a good start. You would be exceptionally lucky to get a coherent explanation.' (Article by the education correspondent, John Fairhall, *Guardian,* 11 May 1976)

Although it may appear to strike just a bit below the belt there is a certain amount of truth in this statement: the question is – where does it lie?

(1) Are art teachers exceptional in not examining the foundations of their beliefs or just rather outstanding examples of the common rule?
(2) Could it be that there is no acceptable philosophical justification for teaching the subject at all?
(3) Do visual artists, even as teachers, tend to be less than coherent about the purposes of their work than other subject specialists?
(4) Is the art teacher's problem due to the fact that his subject has so many facets, that there are so many rationales about what to teach and how to teach it that he finds it difficult to select a single, simple explanation of his role?

The chapters which follow attempt to define the different kinds of potential objectives from which teachers may choose, and in practice do choose, and the kind of classroom activities which may be considered consistent with the selected aims.

If I believe that such an analysis is overdue it is not because I think the art teacher is in particular need of a straitjacket, nor that he should voluntarily cast himself in any self-limiting role. It is necessary to clear the air. The American educator Dr Manuel Barkan, described the British system as 'idiosyncratic',[1] he found that the subject of art was rarely structured into the curriculum in a serious and meaningful way. Dick Field, in an important book, *Change in Art Education*,[2] states that 'confusion and lack of direction' are characteristic in this field.

After the conference of art teachers mentioned in the Prologue, I circulated an impromptu questionnaire which offered, under fairly crude headings, seven possible teaching aims. Forty of my colleagues (about one-third of the departmental heads in the county) were good enough to complete it. They were asked to code the following objectives on a scale which indicated their degree of importance as teaching aims.

(1) To develop art and craft skills.
(2) To offer opportunities for individual self-expression to as many pupils as possible.
(3) To help talented pupils reach their full potential.
(4) To assist as many as possible to achieve success in public examinations.
(5) To cultivate critical and appreciative values to art and culture in general.
(6) To incorporate technological knowledge and problem-solving methods in an examination of the whole environment, as in some form of basic-design course.
(7) To provide, in the art rooms, a relaxed and creative environment as a contrast to the more rigid academic atmosphere of the rest of the school.

They agreed significantly on only one point – that the encouragement of individual self-expression was the highest priority for the teacher of art.

As far as I know, the only real statistical information available about what British art teachers believe to be their duty was recorded in an article by Meira Stockl in an issue of the magazine *Athene* (June 1974). She had suggested twenty-four possible objectives and found that they all found more or less equal support, though there was a clear preference for 'the development of visual perception' and 'the encouragement of imagination and expression'. In the jargon of the trade, her much larger sample proved rather more concerned with the cognitive and affective

[1] 'Transition in Art Education', Art Education, XV (October 1962), pp. 12-18.
[2] Routledge & Kegan Paul, 1970.

elements of the subject than mine, but equally resistant to emphasis on the operational functions. There are very few of the old drawing masters in our schools today.

But the above is all about what teachers *say*, which does not by any means give a clear indication of what they actually *do* (as John Fairhall claims in the article cited above). The fact is that those teachers who were willing to commit themselves to definite aims placed the greatest importance on the one which is the most vague ('To offer opportunities for self-expression') and were prepared to dip, with equal impartiality, into a bran tub of secondary targets. They gave priority to that end which is least valuable in determining its own means. What exactly is meant by giving opportunity for self-expression? With the youngest children, I suspect, it requires little more than leaving them alone in a protected and sympathetic environment with plenty of materials. Older pupils, clearly, need more than this. How much more, and in what form? The followers of the New Art movement never really faced the fact that a maturing and aware young person can hardly be expected to express himself, even to his own satisfaction, if he is not taught the necessary skills to enable him to do this. They even reconciled themselves to the dubious 'fact' that creativity dies during adolescence, consoling themselves by pointing to the originality and, it must be said, charming naïveté, of the great body of work that their methods encouraged.

There is, at the moment a vogue in academic-educational circles for rational curriculum planning (RCP), a formula which attempts to provide a framework within which methods and aims can be seen to be inter-related. It expresses a natural yearning for order in what often appears to be a confused and chaotic curricular situation. RCP requires that every subject's objectives should be predetermined and expressible in measurable behaviourist terms. It would not, I submit, be a very useful determinant for arts courses in which, almost by definition, no one knows exactly where he is going until he has arrived. It is the peculiar privilege of the teacher of art that he may be presented, from time to time, with works which the artist-pupil or poet has produced with a kind of astonished pride. Such works can be original and, indeed, unique; what is more important the teacher recognises that he could never have produced them himself. I doubt if this particular satisfaction is often vouchsafed to the examiner of CSE geography projects! I remember an old seaside postcard which depicted a drunk rummaging under a lamp post for his lost door key; he did not really believe the key was there, but the light was. RCP does provide a kind of light but is not, I submit, the key to planning in the arts subjects.

Nevertheless it cannot be denied that much of what goes on in our art rooms is underplanned and can be aimless and even anarchic. A little rational analysis could do nothing but good. To start from the beginning – what is it all for? Presumably to assist in the development of artistically educated persons, just as English-language courses are intended to produce literate people, science to help people understand the language and methods of science, and so on. I have (in Chapter 2) tried to describe what an artistically educated person might be like, readers may wish to add to or expunge from that list of attributes. But, having agreed on the kind of end-product we want, how do we decide what courses to pursue in school in order to achieve it?

It will generally be agreed that an appropriate course should contain a variety of elements: learning new skills, making choices, receiving, responding to or rejecting external stimuli, experimenting with the potential of new materials, finding new ways of using old ones, relating in fresh and personal ways to the external environment, cultivating personal awareness and finding ways of communicating it to others. 'But', asks the practical teacher, 'I may accept your curricular aims, though they sound a bit airy-fairy, but what should I actually do? What shall 3B be asked to do this afternoon? What about a syllabus?' Is there such a thing as a useful art syllabus – or are there many? If the latter, how does one choose between them? The answer to that question is largely determined by examining the context, not the least important element in which is the teacher's own beliefs and personal abilities. Other aspects of the context to be examined would include the following, by no means definitive list, and in no particular order.

(1) What kind of accommodation is available?
(2) What equipment can be supplied?
(3) How much time is given to the subject?
(4) Do all the pupils study art – throughout the school, for the first three years, in optional groups, or what?
(5) How many teachers take the subject; what are their special skills?
(6) Do they work together in integrated concord or separately, each in his own domain?
(7) Is the subject conjoined with others and, if so, in what kind of organisation? For example, does art exist in a craft context, partnered with woodwork, technical drawing, domestic science and needlework, etc., or in some kind of fine arts grouping with, say, drama, dance and music?
(8) What is the physical environment of the school and the area in which the pupils live?
(9) What is the 'image' of the subject within the school. Does its

head look for a continuous supply of display material of a quality to impress parents, visitors and other staff?

(10) What importance does the school place on external examinations, and which ones?
And so on . . .

It is possible to isolate a number of separate teaching strategies from which the teacher may choose his own, taking into account the kind of conditions listed above and, perhaps, giving him the kind of ammunition necessary to change some of them. Each of these strategies may, in itself, constitute a whole course, but it is probable that a better balance can be achieved by deploying them either in parallel or in some sort of end-on manner. Each has been found to be intellectually and philosophically defensible, though by different people. In almost no school will these rationales be seen operating in their purest form; in almost all art departments they will be contributing something to that complex organic structure we call a curriculum.

I shall call them:

(i) the expressive approach
(ii) the 'high-culture' or fine-art strategy
(iii) the art/craft programme
(iv) design and consumerism
(v) basic design

and try to define them in the following chapters, using, where possible, the written or spoken arguments used by those who strongly identify with each attitude. If these are not available I shall draw upon the evidence of my own experience of teachers who have chosen to work in that particular way.

Chapter 5

The Expressive Approach

Perhaps the first thing to make clear in discussing teachers' avowed aims is that they rarely mean exactly what they say. Declared curricular aims may be simply caricatures of reality. The very term 'free expression' contains within it a host of ambiguities. The art room may well be a more relaxed and 'permissive' place than one in which maths is taught, but this freedom will always have its limits. When the art teacher says that it is his intention to encourage 'complete freedom of personal expression' he expects his statement to imply that there are many carefully circumscribed parameters, legitimate and acceptable ways, in which he will allow this to happen. He will not approve of adolescents decorating pictures of classical nudes with pencilled pubic hair and, if he takes them out to look at an old building, it will be to stimulate their interest in the form, structure, shape, colour and texture of its walls. No matter how naturally expressive it would be for them to write 'West Ham Rules OK' on it with aerosol cans, such activity is not likely to be encouraged.

Ambiguity of intention is built into the whole idea of art education as an aid to personal expression. That great nineteenth-century apostle of artistic freedom for children, Franz Cizek ('People should draw how they feel. . . . How I should like my children to grow up on islands among themselves!') made his pupils operate within a series of extremely stringent rules. He laid down very precisely the desirable size of a figure in proportion to the page and issued such instructions as 'Begin always with the head!', 'Don't mix colours . . . don't use too many', 'Don't copy Nature'. Cizek was progressive for his time and certainly his children made pictures rather than carrying out drawing exercises, but to our eyes a collection of their products appears mannered, standardised, sentimental, and if they express anything it is the artistic taste and cultural preconceptions of their teacher. Even so British art teachers in the 1920s were bowled over by the 'startling individuality' of the works. 'Freedom' is a very comparative term.

Yet many art teachers are being as honest as they can be when they claim that their primary aim is to encourage the personal, subjective, unique, creative act. The trouble is, it is such a difficult thing to do. Children rarely do what you expect. It is quite a common experience for the teacher to offer his class a free choice of subject, usually at the end of term or when he is busy preparing an examination or display: 'OK draw or paint anything you want to!' This may very well turn out to be the lesson which produces the most commonplace stereotypes, the dullest conformity. All the boys may draw, perhaps, boats, and the girls, horses, usually badly and often in a style which shows a regression of several years' development.

No matter how much he favours the 'free expression' approach every teacher knows he must play a more positive part than that, but he will *try* to remain relatively passive compared with most of his colleagues, to refrain from offering too much of a direct lead, and to abjure the notion of expecting the whole class to be doing the same thing at the same time. He will feel the need to stimulate – but not too much; his personality and preferences might get in the way of the pupils' own needs. It is a little odd, perhaps, that a teacher with similar aims but specialising in drama will probably have fewer inhibitions; it is part of his task to 'let himself go', to encourage his students to do likewise. Why does this characteristic difference occur? It is probably to do with the nature of the medium. The actor's medium is his own body. We all move, gesticulate and speak; acting requires freedom to do this expressively and some degree of formalisation in the interest of better communication. In the visual arts there is a permanent tussle, a tension inherent in their nature, between the impulse and the material, the feeling and the idiom, the medium and the message.

The knowledge that this must be so puts the art teacher into a 'chicken and egg' situation. Can he teach without influencing? If he refrains from instruction does he thereby reduce the range of possible choices open to the children by limiting their skills? If he gives a high priority to teaching skills he knows, he is following a respectable tradition in all the expressive arts. A violinist is not expected to express anything very much until he has mastered the technicalities of fingering and bowing; the most gifted young dancer, has to spend long hours at the *barre.* But the dilemma has two horns. Method, to a certain extent, predetermines results. If he chooses to give lessons in, for example, perspective, surrealist collage, anatomy, landscape configuration, architectural drawing, geometrical abstraction, the use of the air-brush or palette knife, or to pick any other pieces of learning from art's precious bag of tricks, is he not telling his pupils what he wants them to do, making them see what he sees, value what he prizes? An out-and-out expressivist may feel that he is in danger of abdicating from his chosen role.

In practice art teachers usually oscillate between the twin poles of freedom and instruction. They may feel that this is an inconsistency imposed by the restraints of the school system and pressures from pupils, parents and colleagues. They may, on the one hand, accept that they are facing one of the eternal and inescapable problems of the artist-teacher. David Witkin describes it as 'schizoidal'. He says of art teachers that:

'Within the academic community they seek to stand by individualism and self-expression and not surrender to the class-teaching, fact-learning mode of educational encounter. Nevertheless they recognised the demands of controlling the medium and of exploring it for practical purposes and they find this very hard to reconcile with the ideology of self-expression so far as the actual teaching function is concerned. The pupil's interests and the pupil's ideas have become of very great importance to the art teacher in recent years but he has not in many instances been able to couple the facilitation of these within the context of a teaching situation that adequately meets the pupil's needs for controlling the medium. The result is that art teaching undergoes an unnatural fragmentation which destroys the integral nature of the activity and loses so much of the energy that unity and integration alone can provide.' (*The Intelligence of Feeling*, p. 105)

What to teach, how much and in what order, are problems for all teachers. The art teacher who favours the expressive approach is likely to see them a little differently. He may well ask himself, 'How little should I teach and, when I do give instruction, how can I see that it is, or appears to be, in response to the needs of the individual child?'

To a certain extent the art work of the younger children, at least, will proceed along fairly precise lines almost independently of the kind of tuition they happen to receive. This has been observed in a variety of cultures all over the world. Elliott W. Eisner made a number of empirical generalisations about children's artistic development, some of which are summarised below. Readers may wish to check if the results of their own experience in the classroom confirm all Eisner's findings; I have marked those with which I do not entirely agree with an asterisk.

(1) The nature of children's art changes in relation to their ages.
(2) It becomes more complex as they grow older.
(3) As children grow more mature their work gains in cohesiveness, Gestalt quality and composition.
(4) Early work is pictographic (symbolic), representational work comes later, in the middle primary years perhaps.

(5) You may recognise the growth of conceptual maturity in a child by the degree of differentiation in his drawings.
(6) For the younger child, *drawing* is used to express ideas, *painting* for the communication of feeling.
(7) Children of pre-school age create common images whatever their indigenous culture.
(8) The human figure is the most common subject drawn by school-age children. (*During secondary schooling?)
(9) Young children tend to ignore the model or still-life subject even when they say they are using it.
(10) Drawing skills tend to be arrested at adolescence. (*Inevitably?)

Some of these findings, including the last, are confirmed in the Schools Council Publication *Children's Growth through Creative Experience.*

'One of the vital capacities of growing children is to form clear images, and in the work of children between 8 and 13 a whole range of meanings and functions is being explored in their image-making. The technical and the expressive often overlap . . . it is between the ages of 8 and 13 that the inner images often crumble before the pressure of external reality and in consequence there is a gradual eroding of the child's personal imagery. Today, the external pressures of the contemporary world accelerate that erosion.'

Most secondary specialists will have observed this change, this 'erosion'. After transfer from the primary school (and this transfer has an effect in itself) there appears to be a qualitative change in the intentions of the child's work. Searching for realism and the attainment of adult standards can, and often does, bring frustration. The teacher will give a great deal of importance to the cultivation of confidence although, if he favours the expressive approach, he will avoid offering short-cuts to success through formulae and overt assistance, tempting though this may be. The ideal of 'realism' in art is a very difficult one to handle. It can be argued that it is a fundamentally unrealisable concept dependent upon the acceptance of a series of arbitrary conventions – but not with an 11-year-old child!

Later on, at about the third or fourth year of secondary schooling, comes the most critical period. No longer confident in his own powers of representation, fully exposed to the values of his external environment, unwilling blindly to accept the standards of his teachers, under pressure from the competing mores of the academic and vocational side of his school life, the pupil may seem to hit a dead end. The art teacher who has devoted himself wholeheartedly to the notion of self-expression may find himself in the same position. Having restricted his tactics to following and gently nudging the pupil on the way the latter wants to go, he finds he has no track to follow – the pupil is not going anywhere. In many schools, perhaps the majority, this dilemma is reflected in the organisational structure itself. At the third-year stage art may well become an option, at the fourth it almost always is.

It is at this point that the teacher may, completely or partially, forsake his previously firm expressive approach and choose to follow another strategy. The basic-design courses and craft-based programmes which have been given so much importance in recent years have emerged very much in response to the supposed needs of these older pupils. And then, of course, there are always the examinations! No matter how many modifications they may introduce, and there have been many since the war, the GCE boards cannot help but emphasise the intellectual, interpretive, analytical and technical-skill aspects of the subject. To be fair to the ambitious O- or A-level student, the teacher must teach to the syllabus in much the same way as his colleagues are working in Latin or geography. The attractive by-ways of personal exploration must be ignored. I know that there are many art teachers who would deny this and point to much excellent (and personal) work which has been submitted to those Boards which include a course-work paper, or allow course work in craft to be sent it. But I submit that much of this material is produced as exercises conditioned by the needs of the compulsory papers, and usually includes something which has been produced in a mock a few months before. The examiners may value expressiveness, but they mark it in terms of technical competence. They can only be concerned with the product, for that is all they see.

CSE Boards, of course, differ from area to area in their requirements. Generally speaking, however, they accentuate the value of the expressive element in art education and try to adopt procedures which enable them to evaluate it. The system of travelling moderators, for example, does make it possible for someone to overview the development of a candidate over a period. In a very real sense they assess persons rather than selected products. The CSE is a teacher-controlled examination and its general form reflects the desire of art-specialist teachers to continue to work in an expressive way without depriving their pupils of the opportunity to earn some kind of recognised status. It is certainly significant, and perhaps unfortunate, that in the larger comprehensives where both examinations are taken it is usual for the chance for personal expression to be given to the less able pupils who are taking CSE. The more academic are trained for GCE. In an ideal world it might be thought worthwhile to reverse this situation.

How would a visitor recognise that he was in the workshop of an art teacher who favoured the expressive approach?

(1) It would probably be a reasonably friendly place, but then art rooms often are, no matter what the teacher's educational philosophy may be.
(2) There would be no sign of a single, homogenous class activity. Pupils would be pursuing a variety of tasks and projects, using different materials, as individuals and in groups.
(3) Children might very well be observed 'doing things wrongly', using tools incorrectly, mixing unmixable media, handling materials in technically different ways.
(4) The teacher will, inevitably, be very much on the move.
(5) The displayed work will almost certainly show little sign of the teacher's selection.
(6) There would be no syllabus, no predetermined scheme of work.
(7) The idea of following a chain of inevitable steps to predictable conclusions is anathema to the expressive creed. It is interesting, incidentally, that the art teacher is specifically exempted from the duty of providing visiting inspectors with a copy of his syllabus.
(8) Members of the department will be likely to identify themselves, and this may even be expressed in the school's organisation, with the other 'expressive' departments – drama, music, dance, movement – rather than with the vocational crafts.

The visitor, upon inquiry, might very well find the teacher rather on the defensive. The expressive approach conveys the deeply held convictions of a large number of artist-teachers and has established its own traditions over nearly half a century. Nevertheless it is under attack by others who favour more rational curriculum planning. Warren Farnworth, a senior lecturer in art, wrote in Colour Review: 'We cannot forever allow the art teacher the dubious freedom to juggle subjectively and haphazardly with the notions of free expression, emotion and feeling, in the vain hope that when they fall to the ground they will form, by chance, the elegant patterns of thought and sensibility which all art allows.' There is no easy verbal rejoinder to this perfectly valid criticism; the expressive approach is based on feeling and intuition about the nature of art and the psychology of children. It has its own internal inconsistencies which are not always faced up to. The teacher cannot even point to the excellence of his displayed work in rebuttal for, by his own beliefs, Kate's work is only important in so far as it communicates what Kate thinks and feels. How can any third party assess that?

I would suggest, however, that there is one question he might put to himself which is valid in his own terms. Could it not be possible that, in his fear of imposing his viewpoint on *young children*, the convinced expressivist may, by neglect, be imposing upon *adolescents* methods not appropriate to their free and proper development?

Chapter 6

The Fine-Art Strategy

'One day, let us hope in the not-too-distant future, we will come to realise that 'aesthetic literacy' is the right of the educated man; just as education is the right of all men' (Dr d'Arcy, head of the art education section of the Department of Culture at UNESCO)

If it is granted that the purpose of education is to assist the development of the educated adult person, and accepted that it is very unlikely that such a person will become a practising artist, it should follow that arts courses should lead at least as much to the appreciation of the work of others as to the encouragement of the skills of personal expression. The main purpose of a curriculum based on the fine-art strategy would be to help as many pupils as possible to reach that 'aesthetic literacy' so much desired by Dr d'Arcy.

The advocate of such a course does no dishonour to his subject when he requires that it should be placed firmly within the common core of the essential curriculum. For him, the aesthetic is classed as a form of *knowledge* no less important than mathematics, physical and human sciences, history, religion, philosophy, and so on. He will claim that its strategies of thought – ways of looking, thinking, describing, recording, analysing, evaluating – are as important to the development of the aesthetic man as reading and writing are to the literate man. He will not undervalue artistic *activity* in the classroom – art education must always contain a certain amount of making and doing – but he will see it as a useful reinforcement of knowledge and insights gained during what is, fundamentally, a serious academic course. He is concerned with traditional standards and shared values; if this leaves less time for sensory training or individual self-expression this does not matter. Indeed, he may believe that much of what goes on in our art rooms under the heading of self-expression is an appalling waste of time, as does Bob Coulter who, in a heated article in *Colour Review* (Spring 1976), writes: 'The pupil derives very little knowledge of art from his years of schooling which are supposed to include art education. In fact, the small amount of knowledge he has absorbed could probably be taught within three or four weeks on an intensive course.'

I have no way of knowing how generally true this statement is; on the whole I would think that it is substantially so. Very few secondary school pupils receive what Coulter would accept as an adequate education in the fine arts, even if they are part of the small minority who are following up the art history and appreciation syllabuses at either of the GCE levels or preparing historical projects as part of their course work for CSE.

Many art teachers feel some sense of guilt about this vacuum in their courses and point defensively to the average intellectual level of the pupils they usually have to teach, particularly at the top end of the school. They do not habitually face classes of pupils who are capable of the rigorous exercise of intelligence necessary to perceive the significance of magic, myth and religion, the findings of archaeology, social history and psychology in the development of art in the consciousness of mankind. Neither are they necessarily equipped to handle such concepts themselves; their training may well have been along different lines altogether. So, for these and other reasons, the fine-art strategy rarely forms the basis for schemes of art work in the schools.

Those who wish to give it more importance do not often believe that such studies are suitable for all their pupils. They feel they have a choice. Either they develop courses which are appropriate for all their pupils, and this may mean, on the whole, practical ones, or they have to embrace the divisive notion of a dual curriculum. This would mean in practice that the 'high-culture' strategy would form the basis of their work with the more intelligent pupils, the others would pursue different aims, such as those defined in Chapter 5, 7, 8 and 9 of this book. Streaming would then, almost for the first time, enter the art room.

It is worth examining the implications of this approach. The notion that there exists in our society a statistically determinable subgroup ('the folk') with a separate culture and distinct educational needs has been forcefully put forward by Professor Bantock. He suggests that these needs are practical training, vocational guidance and education of the emotions. It may appear to have a certain validity, especially to frustrated pessimists working in some sectors of contemporary secondary education. It is no part of my brief to discuss the general validity of Professor Bantock's diagnosis, except in so far as it concerns the culture which the art specialist may be supposed to disseminate. I should, however, like to ask my colleagues to consider their answers to the following questions.

(1) Is it not observably true that the enormous growth in the influence of the media of mass entertainment and information has had the effect of homogenising culture, reducing the effect not only of class but also national barriers?
(2) Whatever the cause, are not the horizontal divisions in modern society (generations) at least as important as the vertical (class) ones: Are our young people more like each other than they are like their own parents?
(3) Could it not be that the conflict between class values, so far as this still exists, have been *caused*, or at least intensified, by this kind of divisive educational provision?
(4) Is it really the 'folk' (the bottom 30 per cent of the school population) who particularly need what Bantock calls the 'education of the emotions'?

Here, perhaps, I might cease to ask questions and make a statement of my own. I have found that it is precisely the high achievers, those who are successfully coping with a highly verbalised, closely structured, book-based academic curriculum, who most need the balance of affective education. It does them no service at all if art is turned into another subject to study like all the others. As I suggested in the Prologue, it is often among the people who ought to have been educated to know better that one encounters the deepest philistinism. This is unlikely, on the face of it, to be eradicated by lectures on art history, aesthetics or critical analysis.

It would be quite unfair to caricature the practices of a fine-art strategy as being composed solely of museum visits, film-strip illustrated lectures and essays on Michelangelo. Art teachers know well enough that there is a great difference between knowing about art and appreciating it; appreciation most closely follows personal involvement. As Eric Newton wrote, 'Every artist knows from experience, but few laymen ever realise, the constant interplay between mind and hand as a work of art progresses.'[1] In all art courses the pupil is expected to spend some time making art, what distinguishes the fine-art strategist is the kind of art he will expect and the reasons he will give for expecting it. He will always try to relate what the pupil does to a sequential study of the nature of art products from the past and present. He will firmly teach techniques in an attempt to get the pupil to appreciate, *from the inside*, the kind of problems artists have to face, and how they have been overcome. One might imagine, for instance, a series of lessons concerned with the problem of portraying depth on the picture plane. How is it possible to indicate space and distance on a flat surface?

[1] *The Meaning of Beauty*, (Pelican, 1952).

The class could be shown examples of ways in which artists in the past have (i) ignored the problem altogether, (ii) found (in the oriental manner) formal ways of by-passing it or (iii) developed, step by step, such conventions as linear and aerial perspective. Such a study would include Cubism and its modern derivatives. The student could then be asked to carry out a series of exercises in one or more of these styles and develop one of them into a full-scale piece of individual work. Other themes might include the use of colour, the portrayal of light, a study of landscape styles, a variety of representations of the human body, and so on. This thematic approach would almost certainly be more fruitful than a chronological one. An art historian who included a fair amount of practical work in his courses could never cover the field adequately in any other way.

Other teachers, specifically the wholehearted advocates of self-expression, could very well object to this kind of procedure, claiming that it could lead to the kind of copying which was characteristic of the nineteenth-century drawing class, albeit in a much more sophisticated form. A writer in the journal of the American Progressive Education Association objected absolutely to the introduction of any form of adult influence: 'There was a time when children's imaginations were nurtured by nature and life. Now they are overwhelmed by illustrated books, trips to Art Galleries and Museums and the like. . . . Looking at pictures, if it teaches them anything, teaches them the art of imitation.' Perhaps it all depends on what you mean by 'children'. A great deal of educational criticism, particularly in the field of art, is bedevilled by this kind of imprecision about the age and developmental level for which certain educational approaches are designed. Anyway, Brian Allison has a short and sharp reply to this apostle of innocent art: '. . . art forms, particularly at the pupil and student level, are mainly derivative and, I would emphasise, *there is nothing wrong in that*'.[1] Reminding us again of the tiny proportion of our students who will become active artists, he goes on to suggest that it would be more realistic if teachers designed their courses to produce sensitive critics, historians, freely discriminating consumers. The advocate of a fine-art strategy would tend to agree with this, though he would probably shy away uneasily at the commercial connotations of the word 'consumer'.

There are three classical critical questions which can be applied to the judgement of any work of art: (1) What does it try to do? (2) Is it worth doing? (3) Is it (or can it be) done well? It might be useful to apply them to this, and any other, teaching rationale.

[1] 'Sequential Programming in Art Education', in D. W. Piper (ed.), *Readings in Art and Design (After Hornsey)* (Davis Poynter, 1973).

(1) WHAT DOES IT TRY TO DO?

The fine-art strategy attempts to provide the potential adult with the possibility of a richer life, to create a better understanding of the nature of human beings as expressed through art, to increase sensitivity and discrimination, to teach the language of tempered criticism and to counteract cultural deprivation by offering to young people the opportunity to share in the artistic inheritance of their community.

(2) IS IT WORTH DOING?

Most (though not all) art teachers would accept the validity of these aims. Some may doubt whether this particular kind of course is the best way to achieve them. Others may believe that there is no such thing as a valid common culture and that the teacher may find himself being the mere transmitter of the standards and values of a dominant middle class. They are not all convinced of the relevance of 'high culture' to the lives of the majority of the youngsters they teach.

(3) IS (OR CAN IT BE) DONE WELL?

This must be for the individual teacher to decide, in the light of his own experience. It may be not possible at all. After all, most of the masterpieces which will form the basis of such study will have been produced by people with exceptional skills and aptitudes, after long years of study and experience of life. Visual artists (unlike some musicians and mathematicians) seem to need to mature, like cheese and port. Can any child or adolescent be expected to enter, more than very superficially, into their world? Is it really possible to convey in school the kind of experiences – personal, social, historical and cultural – that lie behind one work of Daumier or Van Gogh? I have before me a series of children's statements quoted, with apparent approval, in a well-known book, *The Growth of Child Art* by R. R. Tomlinson and J. F. Mills. One boy thought that the Mona Lisa (that most boring of masterpieces) was rather inferior to its reproductions. Another boy described Rembrandt's series of self-portraits as pictures of a 'doddering old drunkard'. Their journeys to London, Paris and Amsterdam seem hardly to have been worthwhile – or could it be that language is an unsuitable vehicle for the expression of a response to visual art? And the fine-art strategy does depend, rather heavily, on verbal communication between teacher and taught. A more truthful record of their real reactions might have been found in the development of their own art work.

Many teachers believe that it may – but not quite all. The following quotation (and it is by no means representative of the ideas of the majority of convinced supporters of a 'high-culture' strategy) seems to me to be the expression of art academism run wild. It comes from a contribution by John White to an Open University course on curriculum design.[1]

'As for creative aesthetic activities, these are often supported on the grounds that they are necessary for appreciation – that one cannot properly love poetry or paintings until one has oneself tried poetry or painting. I know of no evidence for this commonly held view, and I should have thought it easy to find empirical evidence against it, of poetry lovers, for instance, who have never written a line.'

Well, maybe – but have you ever tried to convey the subtle intricacy of cricket to a Frenchman or the elegance of a chess problem to someone who has never handled a pawn?

[1] Open University Course E203, units 9 and 10.

Chapter 7

Through Craft to Art

There can be no successful art without craft, so long as the 'craft' is used to mean skill in the use of materials and tools. On the other hand, there can be craft which does not necessarily involve art. In this sense someone who, presented with a set of plans, carried them out to the best of his ability but with very little opportunity to change the design once the work is under way, is a craftsman. He has a clear picture of what he intends to achieve – the artist can never be in that position. 'I do not seek – I find', said Picasso. Experience shows that these lines of demarcation are very often taken for granted in schools. We have art departments, craft departments, craft in art departments and, much more rarely, art in craft departments.

These days every large art department contains a great deal of equipment which is more commonly found in craft workshops. Sets of woodwork tools, soldering, brazing and welding equipment, sewing machines and looms abound. Then there are the other expensive items of capital equipment more usually associated with the arts. Kilns, for pottery and enamelling, pug-mills, a great variety of printing processes, fully equipped dark rooms – all these are considered almost basic necessities for a fully comprehensive art course. When art teachers attend in-service courses, and I suspect that as a group they have a good record for diligence in this respect, it is usually in order to learn or develop some specialised craft skill.

In a random selection from a number of periodicals produced especially for the art teacher one finds the following articles: 'The making of jewellery; 'Printing techniques with postapaste'; 'Design for drama'; 'Modern embroidery'; 'Typography'; 'Graphics in the media'; 'Architectural models'; 'Make your own ceramics kiln'; 'Exercises in Display'; 'New uses for polystyrene'; 'Soft toys'; 'Kinetics in the classroom'; 'Stone mosaics'. To be an art specialist these days one needs to be able to teach a great deal more than painting and drawing. Book reviews in the same periodicals indicate the commercial advantages to be gained from catering for teachers looking for new skills to pass on to their pupils.

So complete has been the operational revolution within art education in the last twenty years that the subject is often realistically timetabled under the title 'art/craft'. Yet there is no specific identifiable art/craft rationale. Some crafts are always practised, no matter what the explicit or implicit ideology of the teachers concerned. Their importance is taken for granted. Art teachers have almost always been trained in one or more of the art crafts. Pupils, especially those who have no particular talent for drawing or painting, enjoy the increased scope of the courses they are offered. Head teachers value the department more when it produces a flow of permanent or semi-permanent pleasing artefacts to decorate the premises, especially as these are easy to understand and are comparatively free from the ambiguities of fine art. It may be thought that there is no need to objectify aims and pin down purposes when so much good work is being done.

But perhaps we do need to look at the art/craft syndrome a little more closely to see what is actually being done and what it expected to result from it. Some people place craft in the central core of the subject. Henry Pluckrose, a primary headmaster who is a great influence on art education at all levels, insists that no child can live fully in a modern technological society unless he or she has been given some insights into the 'basic processes of mankind'. He maintains that it is the arts and crafts which chart man's progress towards civilisation.

Herbert Read expected great things too: 'The crafts could, more than any other form of education, transform our social environment. As an instinctive revolt against the shoddy products of our factories they could immediately bring into the home an undercurrent of good taste in furnishings, clothes and utensils.' If anyone has to bear the burden of improving the taste of our coming generations of consumers it may very well be that the art teacher has to take a major share. Should we not ask, however, if the enormous proliferation of craft *activities* which entered the sphere of art education in the 1950s is the only way to set about this particular task?

The DES Survey No. 11 (1971) had no doubts about the value of craft work in forming a sense of discrimination in children: 'The process of understanding and evaluating begins with a certain material substance and leads on to a created object. The making of an object demands many decisions and is therefore an excellent training ground in independent judgement.' This seems to be a perfectly acceptable statement yet one wonders if it is always confirmed by practice. It may be that if the teacher takes as his primary aim the inculcation of discriminating and sensitive responses to artefacts he ought to set out to *use* his art/craft sessions with this positive purpose in mind. Free activities in the art room may only serve to act as a pipeline for the very culture the course purports to upgrade.

I should like to digress by giving a personal example of this. Years ago I taught art in a London secondary modern school. Pottery was a very popular subject. Its teacher was a sympathetic person and a fine craftsman. Most of the pupils became excellent manipulators of clay and in their exhibitions the ceramic work was much admired. As part of the preparations for a grand open day I asked the pottery teacher to make the very *worst* possible cup and saucer he could. He obliged; it looked something like Figure 3.

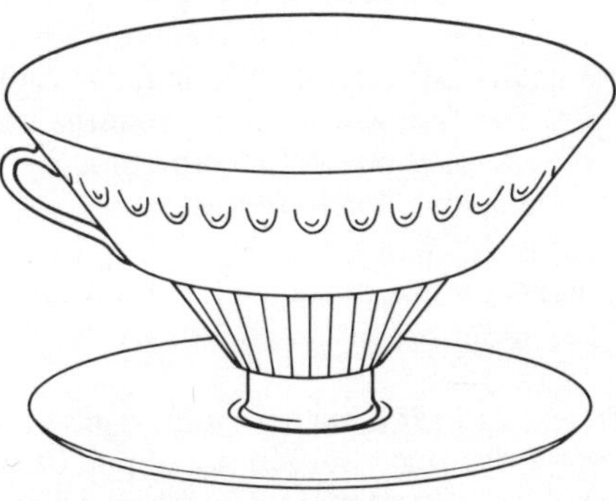

Fig. 3

He had built into their forms at least six obvious (we thought) functional design faults. We displayed the cup and saucer alongside a score or so commercial crockery sets and asked pupils, teachers and visiting parents to give each a graded mark. Our impossibly inefficient models turned out to be the clear favourites. They did, after all, have a certain grace and were charmingly decorative. We concluded that 'learning by doing', though it has obvious virtues, may not be the best way to teach judgement of design. It could be argued that if you want to improve pupils' taste you might as well set about doing it in the obvious way by teaching the principles and practices of design (and face the élitist connotations which such a course might seem to imply). Although craft activities would still play a part in such a study they would serve mainly as illustration and reinforcement; the cognitive element would be most highly valued.

There are other reasons for getting away from drawing and painting. Some experts believe that adolescents, in particular, lose their creative urge and that great emphasis should be placed on craft and design education to fill the gap between child art and that of serious art students. Andrew Nairn wrote, in *The Growth of Child Art*: 'It may be that during this period of imaginative recession and before the arrival of other standards, more satisfaction can be attained by stressing design and the crafts, with a specific task set, and certainly in many schools I find the potters, the screen-printers, the model-makers and the puppeteers showing a better grasp than in the painting at that age.' 'Craft *instead* of art' might be the name of this strategy.

The fact is that the craft element can be incorporated into any of the basic art strategies. The committed expressivist teacher will welcome any addition to the range of creative opportunities offered to his pupils, though he is not likely to value the development of craft skills for their own sake. 'Through craft to art' will be his watchword. He will not necessarily insist on the adoption of correct techniques nor allow the constraints of craft discipline to inhibit his pupils' quest for personal expression. The following extract from the transcript of an Open University broadcast about a Yorkshire primary school, called 'The Balby Street Kids', may illustrate this.

The presenter, Donald Holms, is interested in the somewhat unorthodox way in which one of the boys is modelling the head of a fox in clay. The boy describes his manner of working.

Boy: Well, first of all I get a big ball of clay and roll it up and then I pull the face out. I get hold of it and pull its nose out . . . nose off, to about the size I want it and I get a knife and slit it open. Then I can open it up and do all the inside of his mouth.
Holms: I see, Have you ever thought of building up the head with little pieces? Has anyone suggested that to you?
Boy: Yes, but I like doing it this way.
Holms: And your . . .
Boy: Most of the people, when they do it, they do it like that . . . in pieces.
Holms: But you prefer it this way?
Boy: Yeah, pulling them out, of his face.
Holms: And you are left alone to do that?
Boy: Yeah.

When the BBC Unit went to film this activity they found the fox's head was no longer there; it had turned into a badger.

If craft within art can serve so many purposes this makes it all the more important for the teacher to see that he encourages the kind of practices which support his chosen aim. It is possible that they may not do so, may, in fact, positively contradict it. It would be difficult to defend an arts course which had as its declared aim the encouragement of sensitivity and discrimination if the pupils were happy to produce gaudy and badly registered colour prints or crude and unusable pots. By the same token, the teacher might find it equally difficult to reconcile expressivist aims with a display of pots which the pupil has slip-cast from commercial moulds or of collages, puppets, mobiles, and so on, whose design had come from books or work cards.

A recent factor in the organisation of larger schools could radically redefine the role of art education altogether. In certain comprehensives, subjects have been joined into notional groups. This has appeared to be a natural way of simplifying the school's administrative structure. Art/craft faculties and design centres have come into being. In such conglomerates it is the craft element which seems to provide a convenient bridge between the disciplines. On the face of it this is a simple and tempting proposition. Why should not a needlework specialist use her special skills and experience to improve the quality of a pupil's fabric design and collage work? Does it not increase the sculpture student's freedom to develop his expressive skills by learning to carve in the woodwork room and make his own armatures in metalwork? In return, crafts students would benefit from more relevant artistic tuition.

In time this kind of cross-fertilisation will become more general and may well turn out to be the most fruitful innovation in the field of art education for half a century. Even now there are schools in which this kind of arrangement works very well. But it is useful to look for pitfalls when administrative decisions set up teaching structures which have to be manned by staff who have not been trained to fit into such patterns. During the entire history of British public education the teachers of handicrafts and art have observed quite different traditions. The New Art movement between the wars only served to enlarge the gulf by giving art teachers a rather special sense of identity and destiny. In the 'real world' it may not be particularly helpful to distinguish between the craftsman and certain kinds of artist; in schools the line of demarcation has been fairly strictly preserved.

The division between art and craft is essentially a nineteenth-century concept. The Greeks and Romans made no such distinction. For them there were many crafts and most of them were useful – such as wine making, soothsaying, carpentry and surgery. An artist was simply a special kind of craftsman. This attitude persisted in Europe at least up to the Renaissance period. The mason who squared up the blocks of stone to built a church might, if he happened to show a particular aptitude, be the same man who carved the figures of saints to adorn it. The absolute paradigm of Renaissance man was, of course, Leonardo, who saw little difference in kind between his activities as a painter, court musician, designer of cannon, water conduits and unflyable aircraft. But now we accept the convention that the terms 'art', 'artistic' and 'artist' are courtesy titles which related to the production of special and individually distinguishable articles which are intended to entertain or stimulate the senses or emotions and which are rarely of any utilitarian value. In spite of the efforts of William Morris and his disciples in the nineteenth century, and the work carried out in the Bauhaus in the twentieth, this idea lingers on. Those teachers who feel that it is time to close the breach between the arts and crafts may well have to look at the new courses in visual education and basic design which are now being developed (see Chapter 9), rather than just annexing bits of each other's territory or incorporating convenient aspects of other disciplines into their own curricula.

It will take time; all educational changes do. The public still thinks of art classes as places where fine art is taught. In my own county of Essex a large newspaper has been organising annual exhibitions of school art for several years; it took a great deal of pressure from teachers to persuade them to change the title from 'Children's Paintings' to 'Art in Schools' to allow the introduction of the kind of art/craft work which is most characteristic of the actual activities now being carried out in schools of all levels. Even now those of us who attend the opening of these shows have come to expect from the organisers an annual lament about the dearth of painting in this land of Constable and Crome.

Children know what they expect art lessons to be. 'Art is for enjoyment, it is for standing back and admiring what you have done, feeling around. Expression of your feelings about something. Not being told exactly what to do every lesson' (14-year-old girl). Craft is different. Boys and girls would be very disappointed if they could not eat the products of their cookery classes, wear what they have made in needlework, and take home to mum something which they have put together in woodwork and metalwork, even if the toasting fork does go into a centrally heated home and it turns out to be the third egg rack in the family.

I have introduced these last two examples rather sneakily but they do, rather neatly if not particularly fairly, illustrate the conventional difference in preconceptions between the disciplines of art and craft. The 'craft' approach, on the whole, accepts the traditional principles of apprenticeship – the same principles, incidentally, which used to obtain in the arts at one time but which tend to have been discarded, particularly in schools, during the last fifty years. The traditional handicraft teacher believes that there is a correct order of procedure! First you learn *how* things should be done. The child must practice the use of tools, how to measure accurately, to make joints, and so on. He then goes on to make simple objects which are chosen because they demonstrate the use and practice of these skills. Only later will he be allowed to choose what he wants to make and later still to design it himself. I am aware that the above is a kind of caricature; that many craft departments in schools operate quite differently these days. Nevertheless, it does illustrate the craft-conscious approach which might be used in any practical subject. Many teachers find such a method appropriate in dealing with craft skill-induction in the field of the arts too.

Many (perhaps most) secondary school art teachers believe that by giving their pupils a good grounding in a variety of craft techniques they are laying the foundation for more genuine freedom of expression later. Contrast this approach to that of the primary teachers in 'The Balby Street Kids'. The craft-within-art teacher has to decide where he stands. Will he allow his pupils to *find out*, by trial and error, the best way to handle the media of their choice, or will he set out positively to *teach* what he thinks the children ought to know, accepting that this must mean some constraints, however temporary, to their freedom of expression? If he opts for the first of these roles he may believe that he does so with the approval of Plato, no less: 'You must train your children to their studies in a playful manner and without any air of restraint with the further object of discerning more readily the natural bent of their respective characters.' (Republic). If he chooses the second, more pedagogical, course, he is accepted the dictum of I. A. Richards who, in a broadcast entitled 'Poetry as an Instrument of Research', said: 'Whatever successes teaching as yet achieves are slight in comparison with those which become possible as the question "What should come before what" is really explored, systematically and closely. There is an order, a system of steps, to be found in every study by which the learner's mistakes can be cut down to the fewest and his powers accordingly encouraged to their height.'

What are the factors which will govern his choice of strategy? There are, I suggest, three important ones.

(1) THE AGE OF THE PUPILS

Developmental stages are as clearly evident and significant in art work as they are in all skill activities. You do not ask a class of 9-year-olds to study Dickens or to make sophisticated multi-block lino prints. There may not be one art/craft strategy, but several.

(2) THE NATURE OF EACH PARTICULAR MEDIUM

Modelling clay lends itself very well to trial-and-error methods; if the child and teacher do not like a product it can easily be changed or recycled. Work which required precise pre-visualisation and the continuously careful use of tools, as in most forms of carving, needs a much more considered approach. (Physical danger and economy are not irrelevant issues here.)

(3) THE TEACHER'S OWN ATTITUDE TO HIS SUBJECT

The good art teacher looks for methods which suit his personality, training and preconceptions. Teaching may well be 50 per cent acting, but the role played has to be a projection of the teacher's own nature. False attitudes are easily spotted by pupils in any subject, in one so much concerned with personal realisation as art they can create insuperable barriers between teacher and taught. The good craftsman will not be able to bear sloppy (even if 'creative') work habits; the more romantic artist-teacher will wish to resist the imposition of too many restrictions and externally imposed rules on his pupils. Self-realisation is both a duty and a reward for the teachers of the arts.

In the last resort it may not matter much which strategy is finally selected, providing the above criteria have been thoroughly considered. What does matter a great deal is that the teacher should have established firmly in his own mind the real objectives of his courses and be reasonably satisfied that the methods he has chosen give him a fair chance of achieving them.

Chapter 8

Design for Consumers

Most people never see a genuine work of art in their lives except by accident, on a foreign holiday perhaps, or during the *longueurs* of a rainy day in the city. Great art rarely appears on television and when it does it is usually in prestigious educational programmes about it (such as Sir Kenneth Clark's) or as props in romantic, scandalous stories of Bohemian life. Radio 3 and BBC 2 were conceived as programmes for people interested in the arts; it was recognised that they formed the minority. It might be said (with tongue in cheek) that one of the purposes of a fine-arts strategy in schools is to increase the number of people who might have the confidence and capacity to enjoy more of the programmes sent out on these channels.

But every single person in a technologically advanced society is in perpetual contact with the products of design. It may be industrial design of products made to satisfy human needs and wants or graphics as applied to everyday communications. For every original painting he may come across the average pupil will see (scan, con, take for granted) hundreds of thousands of books, newspapers, magazines, posters, labels and containers. The whole visual environment of an urban community is man-made and composed of objects designed by someone for one purpose or another. We may, up to a point, choose the kind of house we want to live in, select its furnishings and decoration, lay out its garden. The second most expensive purchase a person makes in his lifetime, his motor car, will be chosen largely for its design qualities. No one knows for certain, though many intelligent people have spent millions of pounds in trying to find out, what influences customers to select particular examples of toiletries, prepared foods, electrical appliances, crockery, and so on. when all they have to go on is the claims of its advertisers, the appearance of the product or, in many cases, of its packaging. We are all subject to what Jack Longland, Director of Education for Derbyshire called 'the whole clanging and ubiquitous machinery of mass communications in newspaper, films, advertisement and much of broadcasting'.[1]

[1] NUT Conference, 'Popular Culture and Personal Responsibilities (October 1960).

For many years bodies within and outside education have been asking teachers to concern themselves much more with the activities and effects of the mass media and some schools have taken up their challenge though, it must be observed, most commonly in courses designed for pupils of the lower ranges of ability. Whether the accepted excuse of examination pressure is valid or whether teachers in general believe that the brighter kids can look after themselves in this area, is a moot point.

True, consumer education is no longer confined to the critical analysis of goods offered for sale and the visual and other languages used by those concerned with selling them. There are larger, more public issues involved. A properly educated person ought to be able to question and, on occasion, bring pressure to bear upon aspects of the practical and visual setting in which his life is to be lived. Should certain old buildings be destroyed and replaced by new ones, or conserved for their beauty and historical interest? What attitudes should we expect our Ministers and Councillors to take in relation to town and street planning, open spaces, play areas, trees, street furniture, poster hoardings, the siting and design of large buildings? Citizens in a modern democracy are expected to take an interest and have a viewpoint on projects as large as the positioning of a new airport complex and as small as the placing of a bus shelter. We have a situation where people are able to *choose* for themselves from a wide range of artefacts and, to some extent, *affect* the decisions which control the form of their own habitat. Increasingly it has been seen as part of the duty of schools to help future consumers and citizens to make such decisions widely.

In some schools a variety of interdisciplinary courses have been developed to handle the task; more and more integrated design centres are being built to formalise structurally the importance of the job. Some schools expect the study to be carried out piecemeal, under a wide range of subject headings. Teachers of English have for some time interpreted this duty as an invitation to deride the exaggeration and imprecision of advertising and usually leave it at that. To my mind much of this kind of work, especially that which aims to reveal the villainy of the language of 'the hidden persuaders', has been bedevilled by a somewhat purist and patronising attitude to advertising on the part of teachers who affect to scorn the values of pupils whose home background is different from theirs and whose preferred television viewing is confined to the commercial channels.

Less tendentious, perhaps, is the kind of course now common in many science and domestic science departments, where consumer products are put to the test in the now time-honoured *Which* magazine style. Valuable though much of this work may be, and it is frequently real, relevant and interesting, it has its limitations. The subjects for study do tend to be domestic and rather dull – soaps, detergents, breakfast foods, dyes and glues figure very often in such syllabuses. More significant, especially for teachers of art, is the criticism that this work is usually confined to a study of *function* alone. There is a very strong case to be made, and a new Schools Council Project ('Design Education 11-16') is concerned to make it, that this is not enough.

'There is one terrible trap that workers in the field must not fall into. Whilst there are some aspects of education in Design which may best be handled through the literacy and numerate media, there are also many vital aspects of the component subjects of Design which certainly may not. Crucial to the concept of Design as a main axis of education is the principle that it carries kinds of sensibility, knowledge and skill which relate to the sensual, spatial and motor centres of the brain as well as the intellectual and analytical'.

In other words, consumer education, or an important part of it, should be considered as part of the province of the teacher of the arts and crafts. If anyone in the school is best equipped to help the pupils to understand why their world looks the way it does it is most likely to be the teachers responsible for their aesthetic education. Brian Allison's comment that the right model for art teaching is the discriminating consumer rather than the creative artist becomes increasingly relevant in the context of design.

If the teacher accepts this as a major objective he has to decide how he is going to go about achieving it. There is no doubt that most art and crafts teachers prefer to approach the problem through practical work.

'Almost universally in their responses to the discussion papers teachers of different subjects have expressed the need to allow pupils to gain first hand experience by participation in design activity in its many modes of expression. They maintained that pupils by active participation will develop insights into the problems and have enhanced discrimination through experience and practice. It has been put forward that this is an important means, and perhaps the only point within the whole curriculum, which allows pupils to develop the co-ordination of cognitive and affective skills'.

The great importance of 'learning by doing' is firmly embedded in the credo of every teacher of practical subjects.

What then can actually be done (made) to induce a greater understanding of design problems? What, in particular, is often done by the art teacher, with a wide range of secondary pupils, in the art room?

In a passage quoted at the end of this chapter Ernest Goodman warns the art teacher against accepting consumer education as a dominating end. He is worried about the temptation to impose ready-made solutions to specific problems rather than offering pupils a language and the kind of experiences which would enable them to formulate values for themselves. Most teachers who tackle design as part of an art course take this point of view. Whilst taking every opportunity to encourage their pupils to study the details of their own visual environment they concentrate on inculcating general principles of good design. Much as the teacher of English will get his classes to write in a variety of forms and styles in order that they shall be able to understand and use them in a personal way when they are ready, so the art teacher will select exercises which demonstrate certain basic laws. This kind of work is pretty well documented, but it might be useful to describe a few of the best-known practices to show how this kind of approach works.

Two-dimensional exercises which involve the analysis of natural forms and man-made structures (*à la* Mondrian) are effective and popular and frequently lead on to three-dimensional work of the space-frame variety (though in these days of shrinking capitations this may be found to be an extravagent use of balsa wood). Design problems – flat, low-relief and free-standing – can be worked out to show the value of using limited shapes and colours and the virtues of simplicity and organisation. (They can also lead to the encouragement of fashionable chic.) The concept of tesselation can be borrowed from SMP maths to demonstrate the classical virtue of repetition and the interlocking circles used in the Altair experiment (Figure 4) can stimulate intriguing and subtle variations of space organisation, demonstrate the continuous interchange between figure and ground.

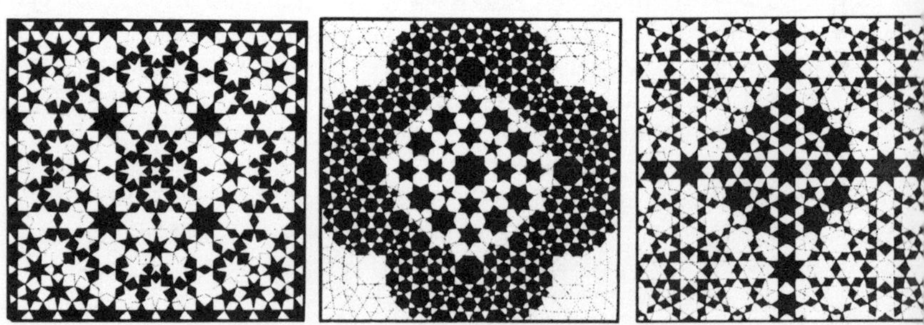

Fig. 4

Kurt Rowland's books on visual education (see bibliography) provide in themselves a full vocabulary of visual signs and symbols which work in the worlds both of external reality and of compositional art. Design courses have been built around this material alone.

More ambitious courses depend for their success on the specific skills and interests of the staff available to teach them. A department may make a name for itself in fabric and fashion work when there are well-trained teachers willing to do this. Some schools offer courses in shop-window and exhibition design. Teachers who initiate such projects are usually aware of the inherent limitations set by the inexperience of their pupils and the unavailability in school of the kind of materials exploited by professional designers. The children are encouraged to simulate the kind of thing they see in the high-street shop windows, in museums and exhibitions, but are not often concerned with constructional problems in real terms.

Graphic design can start quite early, even in the primary school. Children of almost all ages can be asked to design road signs indicating the presence of an ancient castle, an airfield, an army training ground, a garden centre, a nature reserve, or a reservoir with leisure facilities, and produce pictorial (perhaps totally non-verbal) signs to designate various areas and activities in the school.

One interesting communications exercise has been found particularly useful in schools where art and technical departments work hand in hand. Pupils are encouraged to produce story-boards containing only pictures and diagrams to illustrate common technical processes. Subjects for this treatment might include baking a cake, threading up a sewing machine, developing and printing a photograph, safety rules for any mechanical or chemical process. Such cards may be used in the education of younger pupils or used in the planning of films or video recordings. A further imaginative (in the de Bono style) development of the idea is possible if pupils are invited to 'invent', on paper, machines to perform specific tasks like cleaning the house, delivering a newspaper, sorting apples or rocking the baby. Such projections may turn out to be informative, witty, fantastic (for few of them can ever be put together even in elementary prototype form), but they can serve a serious purpose within the design strategy. The student is required to observe actual processes very closely, to analyse all the aspects of the designated task, to select the significant elements and communicate his findings clearly to others.

At the upper end of the secondary school, design students may find the work a great deal more realistic; older pupils are frequently allowed to build objects which they have themselves designed to satisfy an observed need. Some of the art colleges and departments of technical colleges, notably in recent years, Hornsey, have pioneered this kind of work. Students have made toys to provide therapy for handicapped children, designed play frames for infant schools and public playgrounds, experimented with all sorts of ergonomic, functional and aesthetic elements of practical design. In many schools this kind of work is canalised into the production of objects designed to enrich the visual environment of the school by providing seating, display units, small-scale buildings, and so on. Occasionally very ambitious projects are brought to triumphant fruition, very often in the field of scientific instrumentation of an original kind. Unfortunately such activities are very demanding of time, space, money and materials. It is no coincidence that much of the best work of this kind has been carried out in the colleges or in residential private schools as an after-hours activity.

At the general school level (such prestigious projects apart) it must be asked if the emphasis on practical design work does in fact contribute as much as is claimed to the fulfilment of the stated aims of a design strategy. Is it enough to make the kind of objects which can be done in the school situation? Is this the best and only way to teach sensibility and discrimination? Making small and fairly elementary objects in order to learn how to judge the value of large and complex ones (buildings, townscapes, machines) seems to require a great deal of faith in the possibility of transfer of training. This most seductive of doctrines ('five years of Latin will help you to write English') must be examined very closely when it is introduced as the *raison d'être* for any new course. There are three factors which a wholly practical design course may not always take into account.

(1) Pupils do not often use the materials or employ the processes which are used to make the industrial and commercial products they are supposed to be learning to judge.

(2) Although aesthetic considerations are supposed to be as important as functional problem-solving, in practice it does not always happen that way; it is very easy to allocate to the art side its nineteenth-century role of decoration.

(3) Objects made in a school design course may be efficient and pleasant to look at (though frequently one value may have to be sacrificed to the other), but they are not in the same field as their commercially available equivalents because they ignore the market forces which dominate the design scene in the real world. Even in ceramics, where the studio and industrial processes often differ only in scale, it is not easy for school potters to transfer their perceptions of style from their own experience with hand-made earthen- and stone-ware articles into a critical perception of mass-produced products aimed at a variety of specific markets and made from china clay. (The anecdote about the totally inefficient cup and saucer on page 59 goes some way to making this point.)

It may be that this kind of course, whether it is called design, visual education, consumerism, media studies or environmental study, must inevitably have a significant 'academic' component. Sometimes we have got to teach our pupils the things that we know; they will not always find them out for themselves. As far back as 1946 a Ministry of Education pamphlet, *Art Education*, hinted at the nature of the problem.

'The need to teach boys and girls to take an interest in good design in daily life in the wide sense has been emphasised earlier, but nothing has yet been said on the way in which this task should be tackled, except in so far as the actual making of things by the pupils leads to an appreciation of good standards in design and craftsmanship. It is probable, however, that *special methods* will have to be adopted in order to help the pupil relate the experience gained in his art and craft lessons to his environment'. [my italics] [1]

It goes on to elaborate on these 'special methods' as they might be applied to architectural studies. It suggests visits to old and new buildings, analysis of architectural styles, using local buildings as starting points. Why not, it says, bring in local architects and town planners? Time should be given to the discussion of the design of everyday things like furniture, pottery, glass, dress, motor cars and shops. Engineering design can be analysed on site and from photographs and films. There is not (and was not then) anything particularly novel in this suggestion. One can imagine art and craft teachers all over the country saying, 'We do all that anyway! And not only art teachers: a study of the local environment is part of almost every geography and history course, it crops up in botany and biology too. It is probably the most common feature of all primary school work, apart from the teaching of reading, writing and numbers. But there are indications that the contemporary trend towards integrated design education, especially in the new custom-built workshop complexes, can lead to more inward-looking curricula. Teachers are tempted to concentrate on what can be made rather than what needs to be studied. It would be a pity if those wider aspects of design education which call for a humanities-linguistic approach were to become neglected because of an unproven belief that a sensitive sense of values can always be picked up in the course of practical handicraft work.

Design courses are seen at their best when the cognitive, affective and expressive elements are equally involved. Some of the examination boards recognise this and offer questions which require a certain

[1] Ministry of Education pamphlet no. 6 (HMSO, 1946), p. 19.

amount of hard critical thinking as well as art ability. It has always been my impression that O- and A-level design papers in the past tended to select as subjects those which were either culturally desirable or ethically neutral – posters to advertise a Shakespeare production, a ballet programme or a restaurant menu. But in 1974 the Cambridge examiners gave the candidates the option of designing an emblematic motor-cycle helmet. In 1976 they could, and in my experience did, choose to design an insignia for a pop group or a sign for a discotheque. The intention may simply have been to appeal to the presumed tastes of contemporary teenagers, but there was a further effect which may or may not have been foreseen. Students were, in fact, being invited to examine the nature of the kind of commercial image-making to which they were themselves exposed, to examine the motives and tactics of the professionals whose job it is to influence them.

A study of advertising techniques must be inseparable from any curriculum in design for consumers. Simply as one example of how this might be done I include here a sample work card which is used in my department by fourth- and fifth-year pupils who may intend to take the O- level design paper, CSE – or no examination at all.

DESIGN – ADVERTISING Number 7

You work for an advertising agency and are approached by a manufacturer who has made a new breakfast food which he believes will appeal to young people. It contains oats, raisins, nuts and grated chocolate. You are

(a) to find an attractive name for this product
(b) to invent for it a distinctive lettering style
(c) to design the shape and appearance of its package
(d) to design a special showcase to display the goods in supermarkets and anything else you feel might help to sell the product.

You may consider coupons, free gifts, competitions, etc. Look on the shelves in the shops and in your kitchen at home to see how other products have been popularised. Study equivalent advertisements on television. Make a lot of rough (and small) sketches and discuss them with anyone you wish. When you are satisfied set out your design on separate pieces of good paper. Only one of them needs to be in colour and this should be as good as you can make it. Mount your final display on card but keep the best of your original sketches. We will then ask as many different people as possible to comment on your campaign.

Apart from the fact that this work has stimulated the production of competent, attractive, and often original graphics it has also served its purpose by impelling the pupils to examine the nature of the advertising process. The tactics of the hidden persuaders are, to a certain extent, exposed – and from the inside. The children have learned something about themselves and about other people. One girl found that her stereotypical (and beautifully designed) perfume bottle – itself heart-shaped, labelled with a heart enclosing the heads of a romantic couple, coloured pink and called 'Lovelorn', was much admired by her contemporaries, aged 14+, but scornfully rejected by older girls and young women teachers. A boy, seeking to incorporate the maximum *machismo* into his design for an after-shave lotion bottle, shaped it like a Mills bomb and called it 'Blitz'. Sixth-form boys thought it would be effective, but elementary market research revealed that they, and their fathers, rarely bought such toiletries for themselves and that not many females were willing (openly at least) to visualise their menfolk disappearing into the bathroom with bombs in their hands!

A consumer-oriented design course can include a wide range of practical activity and relevant study. It is popular with heads because it can be clearly articulated. Its aims make ethical sense: consumerism, conservation and environmental concern are very highly regarded these days. In the larger schools it may provide an educational rationale which fits into an administratively convenient context. It seems sensible to set up an autonomous design department or faculty, to put together those obvious comrades in craft, woodwork, metalwork, engineering, technical drawing, needlework, domestic science, light crafts, and so on, and find out what they have in common. Will not the art component inform all the others with its concern for individual expression and aesthetic values? Given certain circumstances it may work but the experience which we already have is not entirely convincing. Even when all the participating teachers are willing to work upon common lines, and this is rare enough, it is very difficult to put together a syllabus which suits them all equally. A popular method of tackling this problem is the 'thematic' approach. A well-known anecdote warns of the ludicrous situations which may develop from the slavish adherence to this principle. In a certain school the chosen termly topic was to be 'bicycles'. This quite suited the boys' craft and art teachers but the cookery staff had to resort to the stratagem of baking gingerbread bicycles as their contribution to the joint course.

Most art teachers would agree that the education of the discriminating consumer (in all the meanings of this word) is part of their job. They would be wary of accepting it as their primary objective. Ernest Goodman, headmaster of Manchester High School of Art, warns against consumer education being deflated into a dominating aim.

'If this aim were subsumed by more important ones and the powers of discrimination developed generally and naturally by sound experience of value, judgements of line, shape, colour, texture and structure so that environmental judgements were not only informed but also personal, I would not quarrel unduly with it; it is right that pupils should test their powers of visual perception and aesthetic judgement on things around them . . . but they are also consumers of the landscape, of the architecture and designs of their environment, of the messages – explicit and implicit – of the whole multitude of visual stimuli and symbolic images which assail them throughout their waking hours. The danger is that if this is inflated into a major aim the role of art can be narrowed to limited objectives such as the promotion of *Habitat* or *House and Garden* clichés – a sort of middle-class *dolce vita*.'

Chapter 9

Problem-Solving in Basic Design

Anyone who has read the foregoing four chapters at all closely will have noticed a kind of erosion taking place. After Chapter 5, which is about art as the expression of individual emotion, they chart the way in which this expressive element can be leached out of the curriculum in favour of – something else. The latest and most significant example of this 'something else' usually appears in the curriculum under the title of 'basic design', though it has other names.

Basic-design strategies have evolved under the influence of the most heavily funded pieces of research ever undertaken into the teaching of practical subjects. In 1968 the Schools Council provided over £70,000 for the Keele Project. I have drawn heavily on the published reports[1] on this work, which is more properly called the 'Schools Council Design and Craft Education Project', for much of the material in this chapter. The Royal College of Art was the home of a research project called 'Design in General Education' between 1973-6, and this had been followed by a related Schools Council inquiry, 'Design Education 11-16,' which is intended to pursue curriculum developments in the field of basic design. Only its preliminary planning reports are available. The work, which will involve teachers in Manchester and Cheshire, does not start until September 1976. It has been given a budget of £79,000. There is no doubt that at the highest levels of educational policy making the subject of design in schools is being taken very seriously indeed.

What is basic design that it should be receiving so much attention? In the first place it has little or nothing to do with pure art, whatever that might be. It is not specifically 'artistic' at all. There is a revealing little passage in a paper read by Professor L. Bruce Archer to the Midland art advisers in 1975: 'Since it [this paper] was originally addressed to an audience of art advisers the subject of art teaching is

[1] Schools Council, *Design for Today, Looking at Design, Materials and Design, You Are a Designer* (Edward Arnold, 1976).

referred to from time to time. In almost every instance the word "craft" or "home economics" or "technical studies" or some such alternative could equally well be substituted.' This is integration indeed, when subject names and content may be considered interchangeable. The advocates of design education conceive of it as a backbone to support whole areas of the existing curriculum, as Figure 5 makes clear.

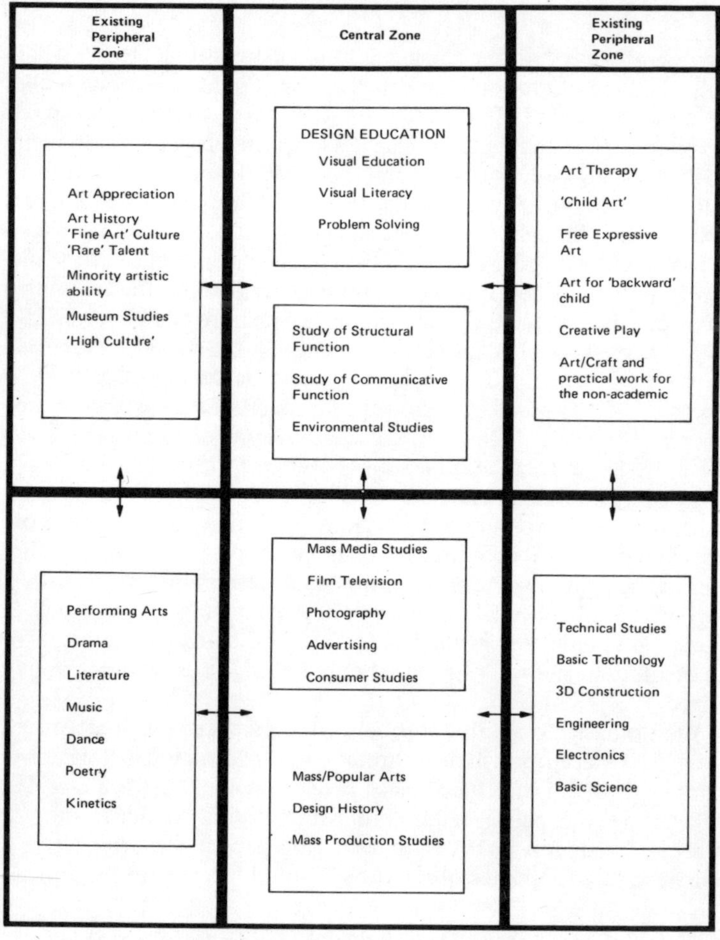

Fig. 5 *Source:* Peter Green, *Design Education.*

Note that free expressive, art, child art, engineering, art appreciation, even drama, literature and music appear in the 'existing peripheral zones'. Shakespeare, Rembrandt and *Joseph's Amazing Technicolour Dream Coat* – peripheral indeed! This may, of course, be a correct and useful appreciation of the real situation of the arts today. Is it not true that in the schools, as in the world outside, art is considered by the majority to be a cultural fringe benefit for the gifted or leisured few? But should this situation be passively accepted, if true? Many teachers of the arts see it as the major part of their jobs to push a concern for aesthetic values and a commitment to personal expression back into the centre of things.

The basic designers say that this is exactly what they are trying to do, but in a new way. Believing that mass production, mass entertainment and mass education have led to the development of a mass culture different in kind from anything which has preceded it, they say that art and, therefore, education in art, must change as well. As long ago as 1919 the architect Walter Gropius wrote: '. . . our task is to make a new kind of artist, a creator capable of understanding every kind of need: not because he is a prodigy, but because he knows how to approach human needs according to a precise method'. Basic-design courses have evolved as part of the movement to educate pupils to use a precise methodology by which to satisfy human needs and desires.

As I have said, there is no area of recent practical education so heavily researched and voluminously written up as this. There is no need, even if it were possible, to give a detailed picture of the many existing and proposed variations on the theme. What follows, therefore, is a sample, or rather a caricature, of the kinds of activities which are incorporated into a basic-design strategy and which represent a complete breakaway from anything we have called art education up to now.

The first distinction is in its conception of the nature of the creative act: Is this philosophy or psychology? Let us refer back to Figure 1, the Witkin-Barratt diagram, the symbolic circular form which represents the unity of creativity. The artist has an idea he wishes to express, conceives of a form in which to express it, manipulates his chosen material and in the process the inter-relationship of these elements produces a state of creative tension out of which the work of art, good or bad, takes its unexpected shape. Like the snake with its tail in its mouth there is no beginning or end to the process. The proponents of basic design believe that the snake can be unrolled and a linear problem-solving series of steps be devised. These steps can be taught, practised and then deployed in original ways. It works like this. Students, as individuals or in groups, are asked to:

(1) Identify and define some practical problem.

(2) Collect information about it and express this data in quantitative terms.
(3) Propose some sort of solution to it. To do this properly they would have to examine existing solutions, assess and criticise their validity, invent a number of possible new answers.
(4) Make a model of their solution. Evaluate its effectiveness. Decide on objective standards by which their success could be measured.
(5) (Possibly) complete a full-scale prototype and subject this to as many tests of its efficiency as they may devise.

To cultivate the necessary qualities of mind to work in this way a whole set of exercises (often called 'games') have been invented. Pupils may be issued with a given amount of materials – paper, card, straws, wire, wood, etc. – and asked to make structures which conform to certain design demands. To erect the highest self-supporting structure possible, for instance, or to make a construction which will support the maximum weight while using the minimum of material. Another exercise might be to enclose the greatest possible space, using no internal supports. We now have the other break with traditional concepts about art, for this kind of work can be *objectively evaluated.* There can be no arguments about matters of taste or opinion. No teacher needs to suspect that a pupil professes to value his own work because 'Sir likes stuff like this', because it fits into some fashionable notion of what is good or bad, or, as I once said in answer to a question about the recognition of real art, 'because the hairs on the back of the neck begin to tingle'. Either the model bridge between two bricks supports 4½ kilos upon seventeen pieces of wood or it does not. This is one kind of work carried on in an art room which can be seen to work by anybody who looks at it. This rare and heady experience is an inducement in itself for art teachers to try some such techniques for themselves.

There is an obvious inherent value in this kind of activity. It offers intriguing challenges to pupils and teacher, whose role becomes more that of a questioning partner than pedagogue (though in these early exercises he may still be in a position of knowing the answers and having tactfully to keep quiet about it). By investigating the properties of materials and structures the children put their toes through the doors of science and technology without being too self-consciously aware of the fact (though a study by the Science and Research Council was not quite so confident about the value of these problem-solving techniques as its advocates in general education hoped it would be). The child has to use his imagination (to perceive the true nature of a problem and suggest solutions), craft skills (to make his models from a variety of materials), and his intelligence to judge the success or failure of his work. Such work does fit the criteria of art in one way – the end product grows out of the activity, there are no pre-prepared blue-prints. It may be an almost incidental by-product but some of the results of these 'games' can be handsome works in themselves, usually in the stark and 'modern' manner – art brutal perhaps. Although a concern for appearance is usually built into design briefs this is often a matter of form, a bob or curtsey to conventional preconceptions. Except in those aspects of design where 'efficient is beautiful' (and it is not always so; we no longer allow architects to assault us with the results of their blind adherence to this doctrine), the aesthetic tends to take first, or second or third, place to other, more practical considerations. It cannot be measured and other criteria can. I have an example before me of some illustrations in one of the pupils' tool books developed from the Keele Project. There are two pictures. One is of a pair of wooden stools with turned legs. The pupil is supposed to compare its design with that of a metal stool, which is shown in the second picture. The captions state that 'these wooden stools are each made of nine pieces of material and have twelve connections' but that the metal one 'is made of only eight pieces of material and four connections'. To be fair, the text only comments on the time, money and materials saved in making the metal stool but the average pupil, I am sure, would assume that this means that it is, in some way, 'better'. Well, I know which stool I would choose – if I could afford it.

A basic-design programme does not remain at this level of exercises anymore than a music course sticks at five-finger drills on the piano and practice in sight-reading. Its essence is that it should be practical; the problems to be solved must be real and relevant. The following are some of the projects submitted by teachers taking part in the Keele Project and reported on in the resulting book, *Education through Design and Craft.*[1]

(1) The design and making of protective clothing for handicapped children.
(2) The design and construction of walking frames for handicapped people.
(3) The adaptation of a motorised caravan to accommodate patients in wheelchairs.
(4) Making a simple musical toy for an autistic child.
(5) The design of a competition kart. (This is a favourite subject, for obvious reasons, and it has a book of its own in the series.)
(6) Designing accommodation for a colony of gerbils. The brief for

[1] Edward Arnold, 1976.

this project required that it should take up as small a space as possible, should be open for general observation by classes, and that it should provide breeding areas as well as plenty of space for the creatures to exercise.

(7) Inventing a method which would help backward infants to learn to dress themselves. The response to this one was a large doll, which had clothing fastened by buttons, zips, press-studs, laces and every conceivable method of attachment.

As the introduction to the new Schools Council Project, 'Design in General Education', says, 'There exists an area of human experience, knowledge and action, centred on man's desire and ability to mould his physical environment to meet his physical and spiritual needs . . . We call this area of experience, knowledge and action, "design".'

Art teachers, generally speaking, are a practical lot; many of them take to this kind of work as ducks to water. Others are little suited, by aptitude or training, to handle it at all. I am one of these. I know that my wife would be highly amused at the idea that I, who cannot put together a respectable bookcase, should presume that I could help my pupils to learn how to put together intricate, complex and original structures. I could cope with the conceptual aspect; it is my unskilled hands which would let me down. Should my department enter the design-education field some form of team teaching would have to be the answer. Either we would need art teachers who possessed the necessary skills and interests or associated craft teachers who would willingly scrap their existing syllabuses and rethink their aims and methods of working.

Such groupings do exist. One of the more impressive examples of co-operation in basic design is to be found in the carefully designed art/technical centre at Pocklington School, a direct grant independant boy's day boarding school in Yorkshire. Here the boys move back and forth between the arts and crafts areas in a flexibly organised way; technical processes are introduced to reinforce and reinvigorate the imaginative art work. In the art rooms a great deal of fairly orthodox design work goes on in two and three dimensions. Drawing is considered to be very important but more as an investigatory and analytical process than one leading to the production of finished works of art. After a close study of natural and man-made forms, at rest and in movement, ephemeral models are put together in the art room, and then developed into more sophisticated and permanent structures in the workshops. A careful balance is maintained between 'art' concepts – and the demands of sound technology. It is important to note that the two teachers mainly concerned in this work, share basic concepts, attitudes and even language. The chairman at one conference referred to them as the Morecambe and Wise of art education, so completely did they complement one another. It may also be significant that the teacher chiefly responsible for the technical side of the work (not that this exists as an identifiable and separate part of the course) was not trained in the handicraft tradition – he was originally a science teacher. An interesting sidelight on the vocational relevance of this kind of study is that teachers have observed that those of their students who go on to follow careers in art almost invariably finish up in architecture, design engineering, graphic design or equivalently bi-polar professions. This is, no doubt, a gratifying alternative to the usual process whereby one's best students are sent to art school where they spend the first three years dreaming of becoming God's gift to twentieth-century art and the rest of the time preparing to become teachers.

It was not until teachers became involved with the various research teams that it was realised just how much importance the subject of design had already attained in schools. It appears on curricula in a variety of guises. 'Design' can be:

(i) a subject in itself;
(ii) a term used to describe joint activities carried out within a grouping of practical subjects;
(iii) part of an art or craft course;
(iv) a substitute (optional or otherwise) for art or one of the crafts, usually in the last two years of secondary schooling.

Art and craft teachers being the kind of people they usually are, (iii) is the most common mode. In recent years the design of school buildings and organisational schemes necessary in the larger schools have tended to encourage or even enforce the kind of interdisciplinary integration exemplified by basic-design courses. In another book in this series of 'Classroom Close-ups', '*Integrate!*', Gerald Haigh knowingly remarks that 'the whole business represents an attempt to add academic respectability to an area of the school curriculum which has traditionally been tainted with low-status craft vocationalism' or, as he does not say, with arty-craft dilettantism. Whatever the underlying motive there is little doubt that design education as (i) and (ii) is gaining ground. You can now take it at A-level. The adoption of a syllabus in design by the Oxford Board, one of the more traditional examining boards, has forced upon it a whole series of new principles and procedures. Co-operation between candidate, teacher and examiner is necessary to assess the often intangible qualities the subject looks for; this examination has had to become the nearest equivalent at A-level to a Mode III CSE. For this reason teachers interested in trying it out are asked to consult the Oxford Delegacy for Local Examinations before becoming totally committed.

Should art teachers allow themselves to be converted to design as they might be to natural gas? Few that I know would be willing to accept that it is or can be a *substitute* for a genuine art-based course; many accept it as a useful added component. It is certainly true that experience in this field is extremely valuable to the most talented pupils who will be entering foundation courses in the colleges of art. It is probably true that art, as we have known it as a school subject, could do with an injection of social relevancy, curricular planning and objective evaluation. Experience shows that pupils respond well to courses which are clearly seen to be pursuing these objectives; they like problem-solving, they enjoy working in groups and they are pleased when the results of their work are understood and praised. How often is the art teacher told that his pupils do not wish to take their good work home because it is never appreciated?

Such courses do not spring, fully armed, into existence. They need very careful planning, the mustering of resources, very many meetings of minds. They cannot come about simply because 'the head saw one in action and liked it', the inspector advised it because 'We have a design faculty so we had better find something for it to do.' It all comes back to the teachers in the end. They must, between them, possess the necessary insights and skills and be prepared to share them at a really deep level. They must *want* to do it. As they used to say in the RAF: 'They can make you do anything. They can make you have a baby – but they can't make you love it!' And a basic criterion for the success of an innovatory course is that it should be a wanted child.

PART III: THE CONTEXT

Chapter 10

Where Does Art Fit into the Curriculum?

There is a very crude way to find out what importance is placed by any specific school on a particular subject: how much money it will be prepared to devote to its development. A scrutiny of the back pages of *The Times Educational Supplement* can be quite illuminating. Heads of departments of 'basic' subjects – English, mathematics, science or whatever – tend to be appointed at much the same scales, according to the size of the school; art teachers may be offered posts under every post-Houghton scale from 1 to 4. Although every single national report from Hadow (1926) to Newsom (1963) has stressed the valuable educational potential of the arts, there is no agreed level at which they should be incorporated into the body of the school. This inequality of status is reflected in any number of practical ways. Take capitation, very much a controlling factor in what may be actually carried out in such a subject, for example. Tactful inquiries among colleagues show that this may vary from £300 to £1,000 per annum in the same sort of school. Basic resources, such as pottery-kiln capacity, show similar discrepancies. Nobody has ever quite established what is the relative importance of the arts subjects to the curriculum as a whole.

In 1943, the Norwood Report suggested that all these subjects (art, music, drama, handicraft) were undervalued and gave several reasons for this neglect: 'When they were adopted into the curriculum they occupied an uneasy position, lying apart from the rest of it; there seemed uncertainty as to how they related to the other subjects, and they themselves did not always justify their inclusion on grounds which carried conviction.' Much of the motive power behind the drive to develop new rationales of art teaching has come from the desire of art teachers to justify their existence in terms which would seem valid to the rest of the educational world.

Anyone who has taught through the period between Norwood and Newsom will have seen many changes in the notional status of the arts subjects: more accommodation, better resources, more full-time and better-trained teachers, more say in the arrangement of the timetable, the acceptance of the need for smaller classes, a larger share of capitation, and so on. Yet the fact remains that no two schools precisely agree on what they want from their art teachers and few art teachers are really quite sure about what they are expected to contribute. Art as a subject can mean so many things to so many different people; it can be justified in so many different ways. Elliot W. Eisner, in *Educating Artistic Vision,* separates the *contextualist position*, in which art education is seen as meeting the general educational needs of the child and being of value to the community and nation, whether these needs are specifically artistic or not, from the *essentialist* point of view, which holds that art has a distinct and valuable contribution to make in its own right. Whilst those people who have chosen to make art teaching their life's work tend to take the essentialist view, it it unlikely that the generality of administrators, governors, managers, head teachers and colleagues are likely to share it. They accept the need for art education, even welcome it, but for different reasons, largely contextual ones. They may see art as:

(i) therapeutic (releasing pent-up emotions, contributing to mental health);
(ii) physiologically valuable (improving manipulative abilities and mental/muscular co-ordination);
(iii) avocational (helping pupils to make good use of their leisure time);
(iv) creative (encouraging the kind of thinking which could spill over into other aspects of the school's work);
(v) a necessary part of a 'well-rounded education'.

The last one is particularly interesting and, in Britain, extremely pervasive. It is best expressed by what I have called the 'high-culture' strategy. Art teachers are beings privileged to hand on to the younger generation the advantages of 'our cultural heritage', thus making them better, happier, more civilised people. In a debate in the House of Lords the then chairman of the Arts Council, Lord Goodman, virtually claimed that exposure to the arts might help to stamp out hooliganism and vandalism!

With all these justifications to hand is it surprising that the situation is confused? Under which set of justifications should art slot itself into the curriculum pattern of any given school? Do schools have curricula anyway? They certainly have timetables; their departments usually have syllabuses. They have complex organisational schemes designed to tackle their educational problems – streaming, mixed ability, introductory years, integrated faculty groupings, option systems, and so on – but I would ask if any of them work in schools which have coherent, thought-out concepts about what they are about and what each subject area is expected to contribute to the whole? Such schools do exist but I am sure they are rare. The larger schools become, the rarer such fully co-ordinated curricula will become.

This is probably inevitable. The traditional and much-prized autonomy of the British head teacher is enviable in its scope, but as schools become larger and more complex this freedom has to be delegated, pastorally among house and year heads, academically to heads of departments. They sit together on working parties, study groups and faculty committees, tactfully refraining from comment on the actual work done by their colleagues, shadow-boxing their way to agreed conclusions. Thus the school menu is prepared, to be immortalised in its timetable. This polite lack of involvement in the affairs of others does not always extend to the privacy of the staff room. Here it can become quite clear how separate subjects, though quite unrelated in philosophical terms, overlap and rub up against each other. Each teacher sees the others' subjects as they succeed or fail in servicing his own. Needlework, handicraft and science teachers complain of their SMP-practising mathematics colleagues that 'they don't teach the kids to measure any more'. Language teachers murmur about the increasing need to teach their pupils how to find Munich, Marseilles or Murmansk on the map. Teachers of commercial subjects lament when their typists' spelling is less than adequate.

Nobody is more aware of his department's role as servicing agency for other subjects and the school as a whole than the teacher of art. He knows how his work is most commonly judged – by what people see. Every art teacher has it implicitly (if invisibly) written into his contract that he and his department will:

(i) keep the public areas of the school decorated with desirable (and this usually means understandable and non-controversial) works of art and craft;
(ii) turn out appropriate displays and exhibitions on open days and whenever numbers of parents, governors or other visitors are expected to visit the school;
(iii) act as art editor to the school and other magazines;
(iv) design all the tickets, catalogues, programmes and prospectuses that the school requires;
(v) be set designer for school plays;
(vi) add to the school's prestige by taking part, successfully, in art competitions;

(vii) take part in useful community projects, where appropriate, thus spreading the good name of the school;
(viii) cultivate in his pupils certain skills, like copying drawings from books, which may be useful in other subjects.

None of these are unforgiveable requirements, nor are their motives unworthy. Every teacher has a duty to his school, as to his subject. These jobs are usually taken for granted. The teacher is right to be worried, though, by some of the *automatic* expectations of the school community which:

(i) consume a great deal of the pupils' time which he would prefer to devote to other activities;
(ii) force him to give priority to certain skills – derivative drawing and lettering, for example – which would not normally figure importantly in his scheme of work, or
(iii) require him to do things which run totally counter to the whole philosophy of art education as he sees it.

It is not always realised how much the decision of one body in the school may affect and distort the activities of others and, in my experience, the art department can be the chief sufferer in this respect. I remember the PTA of one school deciding one evening that an annual school fête would be a good idea to raise money. Each class teacher did his bit but it was the art department which found itself occupying the best part of a term with the majority of its non-examination pupils making posters, stall titles, targets and other fairground impedimenta, even including a set of hot-air baloons. As it happens this turned out to be an interesting and reasonably relevant project (until it turned into an annual bore) but one wonders if any other department of the school would have been expected to deviate from its planned course to this extent. Of course much depends on the nature of such projects and the recognition of the teacher's right to accept or reject them. One art teacher was quite happy for a group of his pupils to become involved in the design and decoration of a wendy house for a local playgroup, positively drooled at the chance for them to make a monster totem pole for the scout troop, but stuck in his toes when his head more or less accepted a commission for the school to produce a noticeboard for the new community centre. He donned his other hat and, as a freelance graphic artist, sent in an estimate for £150.

Up to this point, I imagine, many teachers of other subjects are feeling some sympathy, even though they may have been taking advantage of the servicing function of the art department for years. They know the necessity of defending one's timetable allocation and the importance of being allowed to get on with the job in one's own way. They may not understand, however, the deeper and more subtle ways in which the supposed needs of the school can impinge on the art teacher's conception of his role. Take, for example, his position in the 'competition or co-operation' argument about motivation which still rumbles on in most schools. It has, of course, political overtones: the 'traditionalists' and 'progressives' can dispute their relative educational value till the cows come home. The whole *ambience* of an educational community can be coloured by the importance given to either of these opposing principles. In practice, individual departments and teachers tend to go their own way. Some live by slip tests, mark lists, class orders, merit and de-merit points (all perfectly justifiable in terms of Skinnerian psychology – especially if you are dealing with rats or pigeons); others reject the notion of short-term reward and punishment as valid stimuli and prefer a different atmosphere.

Most art teachers heartily dislike the idea of competitive art. They just do not see that the creative life can be compatible with a sort of Olympic Games of the easel, pottery wheel and the printing press. Indeed one art teacher known to me put down that one of his primary aims was 'to create an oasis of creative endeavour and happy co-operation in a desert of competitive academism'. Yet it is art teachers, of all people, who receive almost daily invitations to enter their pupils' work in commercially subsidised competitions of all kinds, designed to help to sell everything from newspapers to cat food. It is true that they are rarely criticised for ignoring these prestigious affairs but they are also well aware of the public praise which will be given to any pupil who does enter and win a prize.

It may surprise some heads and colleagues to learn that a respectable number of art specialists are not keen on exhibiting the 'best work' at all – even inside the art room. They hold that all works of individual expression, if seriously conceived and carried through, deserve equal attention. Art, for them, is not what goes on walls and plinths; it happens in the heads and hearts of those who have been involved in its making. Lest I should be accused of being idiosyncratic about this matter I should like to quote what Ernest Goodman, headmaster of Manchester High School of Art, said about the danger of what he called the 'genius syndrome':

'More insidious is the assumption that unless a pupil can produce artefacts of an obviously superior kind which will grace the wall, no visual or aesthetic progress has been made by him, and the sooner he drops art to concentrate on something useful, where his progress can be measured objectively, the better.' (Collected papers of the Association of Art Advisers).

It is very noticeable that in most of the writing about art in education the word 'justification' peppers the page. The Norwood Report ('they themselves [*the arts*] did not always justify their inclusion on grounds which carried conviction . . .'), Elliot W. Eisner ('Let's look at the contextualist argument . . . and identify the number of orientations that have and can be used to justify the place of art in education'), and the inspector quoted in the Prologue of this book who asked his teachers to give him ammunition with which to fight for the resources they felt they needed to keep going. It is worth remembering that a modern art/craft course cannot be run on the cheap – you cannot get by with one set of textbooks, a few sticks of chalk and one exercise book per pupil.

This struggle for a subject to find its proper place in the sun is, of course, nothing new. Science had to fight its way into the curricula of the board and public schools of the nineteenth century, handicrafts into the grammar schools of the mid-twentieth. But surely, you might say, the battle for art in schools was won years ago. It appears on every school's timetable; its accommodation, staffing and equipment are often lavish compared with that provided for other subjects. This is true. The struggle is not so much to get recognition that the subject exists but to persuade people that it is of more than peripheral significance; that if schools purport to encourage the progressive development of 'persons' (and are we sure they do?) then much of the stuff of our civilised form of life can be experienced in activities which take place under the heading of art and craft. Properly devised, arts courses ought to take their place very near the centre of any liberal curriculum. Instead of which there is still a great deal of truth in the following statement which prefaced an article on art education in the *Sunday Times:*

'. . . art classes in schools are still widely regarded as a kind of lunatic asylum where the children get rid of their creative impulses so they don't disrupt the serious part of education'.

I hope I have not anywhere given the impression that head teachers I have known have been inimical to this concept of a central role for the arts. They have read the reports; they are familiar with the sophisticated analyses contained in the work of curriculum philosophers and designers; in spite of external pressures from employers and parents for more 'useful', 'relevant' and vocational courses they have stuck to their guns. Many of them, I know, search for ways in which young people can be helped to become aware of aesthetic values by infusing the whole life of their schools with the joyful contemplation of the world of structure, form, colour, texture and meaning, and encourage their children to engage in all sorts of creative activity whenever the natural opportunity occurs. Anyone familiar with the work of Sybil Marshall in her one-teacher East Anglian village school or that carried out in West Riding primary schools under the beneficent influence of Sir Arthur Clegg cannot help but be impressed. The task is perhaps not so very difficult in small schools. If the head knows what he wants and can gather like-thinking staff around him, seeming miracles can take place.

In the very large schools it is another matter. Subject policy is very much in the hands of the individual specialists. As I have tried to show earlier in this chapter they may not be able, through preoccupation, pressure of work or sheer narrowness of vision, to perceive or care how their separate practices sombine to form the school's curriculum. It was once said that every head of department ought to accompany one child through one day's work in order to see how the school looked from the consumer's point of view. Every school embodies certain values, has its curriculum, whether it is planned or not. If the art teacher believes that the kind of work he is doing with the children is of special value and that it requires recognition and support he will have to make his case and keep on making it in whatever corridors the power lies. Art teachers are notoriously bad at this game. I spent some time recently in three schools, in each of which my colleagues referred casually to 'the people down there/out there/at the top' having an undue influence on their work. None of them had any plans as to what to do about it – it was a fact of life. The 'art room oasis syndrone' may be a comforting response to a frustrating situation but it does not advance any causes and there is till a cause to be fought.

It is necessary for teachers of art to recognise that:

(1) Their subject has a unique and irreplaceable importance in the experience of the growing child.
(2) It is an essential part of any form of balanced curriculum.
(3) It may very well be necessary to insist on this valuation.
(4) The administrative structures within a school will reflect or influence the school's expectations of the subject and this should be borne in mind when changes are planned.
(5) If art is to be an integral part of the school curriculum it is part of the art teacher's duty to see that his own objectives are clear and generally understood.

He might carry on his banner the words of John Dewey: 'The moral function of art itself is to remove prejudice, do away with the scales that keep the eye from seeing, tear away the veils due to wont and custom, perfect the power to perceive' (*Art as Experience*).

Chapter 11

Teachers of Art

Even in these days of dress freedom for staff in schools, art teachers have a tendency to look different from the rest. At one time it was floppy bow ties, then corduroys; now the women may opt for tee shirts and jeans and the men incline to denim. This is not a general rule, of course, but if any schoolmaster still exists who resembles Giles's famous 'Chalkie' it is unlikely to be the art master. Is the above description irrelevant and disputable caricature? It may be so, but it has some basis in reality. People do dress to their roles and the part of the art teacher seems to require some degree of permitted eccentricity of dress and manner. Indeed, a questionnaire administered as part of one Schools Council study (reported in *Arts and the Adolescent*, Working Paper no. 54, referred to elsewhere in this chapter) showed that strong 'subject' stereotypes do exist in teachers' minds. This picture of the teachers of arts subjects was one of them: sartorial nonconformism and assumed low academic status were given by most teachers as the reasons why art teacher do not rise high in their profession. And any casual glance at a table showing a comparison between them and other teachers (of languages, sciences, humanities, or even PE) show how poorly they are represented at head teacher and deputy head level. Before leaving this questionnaire it might be interesting to remark upon another of its findings. Art teachers were thought by their colleagues to favour child-centred approaches to teaching. This was not criticised, indeed the other teachers liked to think that they too operated in this way, but it was given as another reason for the limited career opportunities open to a teacher of the arts.

If art teachers are regarded as different there surely must be a more important reason for this attitude than the clothes that some of them wear and a professional approach which others wish they shared? I submit that there are, in fact, two significant factors which distinguish them from the rest of the school's staff population. One concerns the type and status of their training, the other the intrinsic nature of their subject and their relationship with it.

Art teacher training tends to be very highly specialised indeed; most art teachers go into schools equipped only with the particular knowledge and skills which apply to their subject.

Many of their colleagues move fairly easily within groups of subjects or even switch disciplines either in response to duty or to career prospects, but art teachers tend to stay strictly inside their own fields of competence. In a secondary school this may be no great disadvantage; specialisation is the order of the day anyway and some of the generalised expectations of more academically trained teachers have always seemed to me to be quite unjustified. Who really puts into practice the aphorism that 'Every teacher is a teacher of English' and what do real English teachers think of the assumed facility of their subject? But the complete specialisation of all the teachers of art, music and drama reinforces the sense of separation between arts teachers and the others.

Art teachers are also very different from each other. There are so many ways of entering the profession, so many different kinds of training, that, especially on first appointment, it is difficult to know what to expect from any particular person. There are at least six different routes to qualification. Only two of them, the first and last of those listed below, will give the not-always-relevant kudos of a degree, and degree status is still to be valued both in relation to a teacher's career and the contribution he is allowed to make to the general curriculum of the school. This is beginning to matter again. A few years ago the non-graduate art teacher in a grammar school did not expect too much consideration; he took the post knowing that his subject came low in the pecking order anyway. But in the secondary modern schools where most teachers were certificated he could compete on pretty equal terms. Indeed the various ways in which he could qualify for degree equivalence could give him a slight sense of superiority over his colleagues, if he happened to feel that way. Now comprehensive schools are taking over he has dropped down the competitive scale again for, no matter how often it is officially denied, degree equivalence is not in any terms other than financial as valuable as a proper degree.

How may one qualify to become an art teacher?

(1) By a degree from a university of CNAA, plus, since 1947, a Postgraduate Certificate of Education taken at university or in a college of education.
(2) With a degree equivalent followed by a Postgraduate Certificate or an Art Teacher's Diploma followed by an Art Teacher's Certificate, taken at a specialist college.
(3) With a College of Art Diploma followed by the successful completion of a course at a college of education (almost always for one year).

(4) Art Teacher's Certificate, taken at a specialist college; followed by a year's college of education course.
(5) Teacher's Certificate, taken at a college of education.
(6) By taking a B Ed.

Only if he has followed routes 5 or 6 can the entrant be said to have been preparing himself full time for the general job of teaching. It is true that this could also be said about graduate entrants into teaching in other subject areas. There are plenty of young men and women who only decided that they intended (or needed) to become teachers towards the end of, or after they have completed, their degree courses. Traditionally this is not supposed to matter very much. In many schools a degree in sociology, economics or law has been accepted as the appropriate preparation for a successful career in teaching geography, history or religious education. This is not entirely a question of convention, usage or academic snobbery – there is a sense in which all the arts subjects at this level interrelate. But college of art courses are so practical, so individual, so idiosyncratic as between one college and another and between the chosen pursuits of individual students that their products vary a great deal.

Neither can it be assumed that an arts main student at a college of education is being thoroughly prepared to *teach his subject.* This may be a temporary phenomenon brought upon by the contemporary drive to interlock these colleges with their neighbouring technical colleges. It does sometimes seem that their art specialists (in particular) are tending to emphasise their roles as purveyors of personal education in conscious or instinctive competition with their opposite numbers in the specialised departments of the technical colleges. Some of them appear to be more concerned with producing artists than teachers.

Every specialist teacher is, in a sense, the servant of twin disciplines. The science teacher, for example, must have qualities and abilities which relate to the nature of science, and others which help him to become a good teacher. Furthermore, in the hands of a good practitioner, each subject has its own style. A truly capable art teacher will teach his subject in an 'artistic' way. His curriculum planning, classroom practice and evaluation processes will reflect the values of his special approach. The appropriate balance between pedagogic and practical abilities may not be constant; it may vary, not least in relation to the ages of the children being taught. Younger children need sympathetic and reasonably well-trained *teachers* who do not have to be particularly artistically inclined. Francis Bacon would be an expensive and ineffective luxury if he were to be asked to teach art to primary school children. Higher up the age range it is necessary for the teacher to possess a fairly high degree of competence in the creative skills. Much of his teaching will be by example; he will be expected to show his more sophisticated and ambitious pupils exactly how things are done. This may include a variety of highly technical processes. Within secondary schools there is a big difference between the requirements for a successful teacher of younger pupils and those demanded and needed by fifth- and sixth-formers. There are many teachers who can very successfully cope with either but not both of these demands. I know personally several art teachers who admit, privately, that though they handle first- and second-year groups very well they feel they have neither the abilities nor the training to extend the older pupils. Others feel exactly the opposite and are much more at home with older, examination-conscious classes. In a largish art department it should be possible to deploy them in such a way as to maximise their special contributions, but all sorts of reasons – block timetabling, status associated with exam work and seniority are not least of these – usually make this impossible. Still, as every head teacher knows, the problem of arranging things so that each teacher gets the chance to do what he does best is not entirely confined to arts subjects.

My second reason for maintaining that art teachers are in fact different from most of their colleagues is more controversial. I will state it as bluntly as I can, then try to defend it.

Art is indivisible. It is impossible to conduct an art class in school without looking over one's shoulder at the nature of art, culture, design, or whatever in the world outside, to have opinions about the values expressed therein. There is a belief (rather outdated now, I believe) that in growing up children recapitulate the history of the human race. It often seems to contain a kind of truth when you look at their art work.

In most art rooms you will find pieces of sculpture which irresistibly remind you of African, Asian or Aztec work, pots which could have been made by South American Indians, painting which reflect the forms and motivations of ancient Egyptians, Red Indians, eighteenth-century limners or the most modern of abstractionists. A great deal of this is quite unconscious; the child is responding to the demands of his medium and the impulse of his desire to communicate feeling in an almost inevitable echoing of historical forms. Sometimes, of course, it is carefully worked out. And why not? There is a sense in which all art is derivative, each new idea borrowed [from its predecessors] and developed into a new originality. I have happy memories of three third-year boys who presented themselves before an open day with a sheaf of pencil sketches based on details from Picasso's *Guernica.* Fortified with flasks of coffee and sandwiches they worked for seven solid hours on an eight- by four-foot mural entitled *The Destruction of Colchester by Boadicea's Army* in their chosen style, patiently explaining to dozens of bemused visitors exactly what they were doing and why they were doing it. When the art teacher says, 'Let me know what you are trying to do and let me help you achieve it' there is no invisible circle restricting what may come about, or the sources which inspire it.

I do not want to appear biased or unfair to any former or present colleagues but I am not convinced that this is the situation in other, more academic subjects. These have always seemed to me to require a theory of *acceptable limitation*: 'This is as far as we can expect to go at this stage with these pupils.' It springs from necessity: you do not teach the binomial theorem to second-year C streamers. Yet it does make the subject in school different from its 'real' self. A mathematics teacher often knows very well that he is teaching mensuration, not maths. A history teacher in his private capacity may understand that history is 'an argument that goes on for ever', 'tales told by victors about the vanquished'; it does not stop him following a chronological course, based on a series of textbooks which roll through the history of a limited area of time and space conveying the concept of 'facts' with all the authority of an AA road map. This manner of working accepts the limitation, seeing most school work as a kind of preparation for the real stuff which the pupil will be able to comprehend at some undefined later date – in the sixth form or on a degree course for example, should he get that far. Sometimes the truth itself is concealed by this doctrine of acceptable limitation. I well remember starting a physics course, about 1936, by learning a series of statements, one of which was that 'the atom is the smallest indivisible particle of matter'. Yet two years before, Fermi had succeeded in splitting the atom and in the year that I left school he had initiated the first nuclear chain reaction in a Chicago tennis court. Did my science teacher know about it? If he did, he did not tell us. How many so-called educated people discovered, as the bombs exploded over Hiroshima and Nagasaki, that the very basis of one of their subjects had not, in their lifetime, ever been a fact at all?

I have said that art teachers are more or less obliged, by virtue of their interests and training, to be concerned with the world of art outside school. The majority of them, whether they admit to using pre-planned syllabuses or not, are prepared to introduce new ideas at the drop of a hat. A visit to an art gallery, zoo or museum, a field study trip, some local event like a Guy Carnival or the arrival of a fair, even building work on the school site, will give the teacher a chance to modify his courses. Opportunism of this kind is a valuable asset to the art teacher. He may not always be a practising artist. Working Paper no. 54 comments, with some deprecation, that: 'The extent of arts teachers' involvement in the world of art is not easy to assess but the impression we have is that the teacher who practises his art is not as common as we might expect – indeed few teachers are able to find the time to keep abreast of current developments in the field.' Considering that the same report records that 60 per cent of the teachers investigated had to work outside the timetable in order to complete what they would regard as their normal teaching programme and that 80 per cent of them were involved in running extracurricular activities, this can hardly be surprising. It is a little remarkable, perhaps, that the study group found it worth while to investigate the extent of the average art teacher's external related activities. I would guess that more of them do some kind of private art or design work than, say, science teachers do experiments at home, English teachers write books or language teachers use their learning other than on an occasional holiday.

What might have been worth examining is the extent to which art teachers tend to come late to the profession, breaking the school college/university, schools syndrome which is so common. Frequently they bring a great deal with them.

The following is a fair sample of some very successful art teachers known to me.

P. entered the grocery trade and became a shop manager. All his adult life he had been interested in art/crafts, developing a high degree of skill in jewellery, enamelling, glass-making and pottery, until, in his late thirties, he decided to enter a college of education. He took his teacher certificate with art as a main subject and entered a secondary modern school. He attends more practical in-service courses than any other teacher I have known and runs a very profitable business in making intricate and expensive art objects. He is now head of his department and though he will admit to no great expertise as a verbal communicator he achieves considerable success in a particularly difficult school because of the respect he earns for his superb personal ability and knowledge of his craft.

S. followed a fine-arts course to NDD and went into advertising. During the entire period of her education she had no intention whatsoever of becoming a teacher. After four years in which she did very well in her advertising job she moved into an area where, as she says, 'everybody else seemed to be an art teacher – it seemed a handy and useful thing to do and fitted in very well with being a mother'. In time she attended the London University Institute of Education, as a mature student found the work very much more valuable and interesting that the other students seemed to, took her ATC (Art Teacher's Certificate) and entered a secondary grammar school. It was only after three years in the job that she knew that 'teaching was exactly what I had always wanted to do'.

R. took an NDD equivalent course at a provincial art college and, without regret, failed what was then known quaintly enough as the 'pedagogy' paper. He spent a decade becoming an artist who exhibited in many galleries in this country and overseas but one who, like the majority of his kind, had to earn cash to keep body and soul together. Sometimes it was in art-associated activities like stage design and scene painting, but it also included going around on a motor-cycle installing patent devices for killing flies in butchers' shops. He was virtually forced into becoming a teacher when he married and had children and needed a regular source of income. He attributes his success, and this is undoubted, to the fact that he is, and his pupils know that he is, fully involved in the world of art. His enthusiasm and understanding of this world (and, in scholastic terms, only this world) are infectious.

These three are artist craftsmen who became teachers. Their specialist qualifications apply only to their subject; they are never timetabled to take any other. Another thing that they have in common is that their approach to teaching is a great deal more teacher-centred than that of the stereotypical art teacher is commonly supposed to be, though the degree varies. They have all learned their trades and feel committed to teach them. None of them is an out-and-out expressionist though each would be keen to allow any particularly determined child or group to go its own way from time to time. This attitude is even more characteristic of my fourth representative.

B. took a BA in fine art at Newcastle College of Art ('My headmaster insisted that I should go for a degree; I don't think it has made much difference to my teaching but it was good for my status') and followed it with a Diploma of Education. There he came under two very strong (and contradictory) influences. Lawrence Gowing showed him that A-level success in art may have indicated a certain facility, but no more. He had to learn to paint. Victor Pasmore was influential in a breakaway movement which concentrated on developing the comparatively new ideas about basic design. Both these concepts have influenced his teaching objectives. He knows what skills his pupils need to learn and sets about teaching them. He is keen to introduce basic-design courses and is trying to organise one, but the idea has, so far, foundered due to his inability to find craft teachers who are willing to lose a certain degree of their departmental autonomy in pursuit of wider, unproven aims.

D. spreads her net a little wider. Although the holder of an ATC and the nominal head of an art department she works as much as possible in co-operation with the other teachers of the expressive arts, notably music and drama. An enthusiast for spontaneity and personal realisation, she consciously sets out to balance the rest of the school's curriculum by 'providing one small area of experience where problem-solving depends on individual thought, effort and activity – not on retention and recall of pre-set answers as given by authority'. Very much an apostle of the art as process rather than product school and a bit of an educational iconoclast, she often finds her work misunderstood by her colleagues.

In all this group I confess to being an anomaly. I am the only one who thinks of himself as a teacher who happens to have chosen art as his medium. I used to be, and have always been until recently, a practising painter. But art was only one of four subjects which I took for my teacher's certificate and, as it happens, it was one subject that was taught very perfunctorily in my college. It may be for this reason, though I doubt it, that, while holding the headship of an art department for many years, I have also taken classes in French to O-level, helped to design a published Mode III English course, taken a keen interest in all kinds of integrated syllabuses and have become professional tutor to my school.

The actual range of art teachers is much wider than my small sample suggests. I often wonder how head teachers and appointment boards make their choices among them. In the contemporary situation, with jobs scarce and applicants many, selection must be becoming more and more difficult. How can you find out in a short interview, even if you know the language, whether an applicant is an expressivist, an advocate of art appreciation, a good or bad craftsman, a problem-solving basic designer, or a complex mixture of all of them, which is usually the case? Something can, perhaps, be learned from samples of work. Of all teacher-applicants it is often the art teacher alone who is expected to bring with him a bulging portfolio of pupils work or, if he is a potter, a box of pots. One of the least dignified aspects of an art teacher's job application is when, after his interview, he has to repack all his bits and pieces in the newspaper wrappings which are strewn around him. Of course, these days colour transparencies can be used but I defy any layman to extract much valuable information from squinting through these tiny apertures at the light. And are these demonstrations of any value? Naturally they are made up from the best pieces of work available, usually the work of naturally talented children; can they be expected to tell one very much about the general work of the teacher himself? I am not aware that teachers of more academic subjects are in the habit of bringing with them to an interview a pile of exercise books belonging to their brightest and neatest pupils.

I wonder, too, if heads are ever quite clear in advance what kind of art teacher will best fit into the curricular pattern of their schools. When the vacancy is for an assistant in a large department it is usual to consult its head whose general preoccupation will be to choose a member to fill a team, but when it comes to choosing a departmental head from outside, what then? Who knows what unstated criteria are brought to bear? As Working Paper no. 54 states, in several different ways, 'the arts have always been dogged by misunderstanding and misconception as far as their educational function is concerned . . . popular disregard of the arts in school arises not only from a sense of their irrelevance but also from a strong suspicion that they are actually dangerous; socially disruptive and morally ambivalent.' I am happy to say I have never met a head teacher like one quoted in the report who seemed to feel that dancing, pop music and *unexplainable art* contributed a great deal to the deterioration of the moral fibre of the nation. But, who knows, someone, somewhere, may be applying for a post to teach a subject which is considered in these terms.

Chapter 12

Evaluation

Evaluation is an integral part of the teaching process. It is necessary for any teacher to step back from time to time, have a good look at what he has been doing and decide, as objectively as possible, whether he has been on the right lines or not.

> To rise from a zero
> To Big Campus Hero
> To answer these questions you'll strive
> Where am I going?
> How shall I get there?
> How'll I know when I've arrived? (R. F. Mager)

This is all very well as long as one can be sure of the proper standards to apply. It seems to me that the assessment of progress, whether of an individual child or a whole class, is about the most difficult task the teacher has to face and the one that is commonly done the least well. Yet I am not convinced that many teachers take the same view.

We do a lot of testing. There are short-term tests which are designed to find out how much a child has retained of his recent lessons or whether he did his homework last night, and the school year is punctuated by those more formal affairs, the examinations, which call for special rooms, watchful invigilators, disrupted timetables and a great deal of time for preparation, participation, marking and inquests. The results of these constitute the main basis of the school's evaluation process. By their results pupils are praised and promoted, blamed and kept down; parents are worried or elated; career prospects are enlarged or denied. These days some schools and many teachers try to take some of the examination sting away by using some form of continuous assessment, though students experiencing this may look upon it as a form of continous ache. Whatever the method of judgement, every now and then the pupil takes home the authoritative evaluation of his progress – his school report.

Many schools still use the old type of report form familiar to all our childhoods, with one line given to the assessment of a year's activities in each subject. On the face of it, it looks factual and fairly informative. 'HISTORY . . . 27% . . . 16/30. John could have done better in his examination.' What it does not tell its readers is the top, median and range of test marks in John's class (which clarify the significance of his own score), where his group stands in comparison with others of the same age, *why* he did not do better in his examination, whether he worked well or badly during the period, what special conditions (change of staff, for example) might have influenced the progress of John and his fellows. What is never stated, indeed cannot validly be assessed, is the standard of the tests which have been set. Parents are given to drawing quite unwarrantable conclusions from the small amount of information they actually get. They compare John's 27 per cent with his last year's 50 per cent and give him a clip on the ear for slacking, not realising that such comparisons are meaningless. Teachers are not always immune to this kind of sweeping judgement either. How many teachers are guilty of groaning in the staffroom that '2A aren't a patch on last year – you should see their exam. results?' In an educational world in which the most heavily validated and reliable tests (of whatever IQ tests are supposed to measure), carry a potential 12 per cent error, we ought to know better.

It is now being fairly widely recognised that it is not very sensible (or perhaps even ethical) to try to quantify a pupil's performance in precise numerical terms. We now have report sheets which may look something like this:

'MATHEMATICS Effort B+ Attainment C
Jane has had a lot of ground to make up after her absence but is trying hard. She is attentive in class but her homework shows that she is still unable to understand some of the basic ideas of the subject. She is a helpful and co-operative member of her Tutor Group'

The extra space given to 'comment' may cause extra work for specialist teachers, form tutors and house or year heads, but this method of reporting does go a long way towards considering the child as an individual in the context of the school.

Before passing on to consider the relevance of all this to the assessment of art work in particular, it might be worthwhile to ask whether this kind of activity is exactly what evaluation is all about. Definitions will help.

Evaluation is the process of making value judgements about educational phenomena.
Testing is one procedure for obtaining the data for making these judgements.
Grading is the process of assigning a symbol (mark, percentage, class position, letter- or number-grade) which stands for this judgement of quality relative to some stated criterion.

Testing and grading can be made to look reasonably simple, though in fact they are not. Certainly, true evaluation of a pupil or course is very difficult indeed. It involves the judgement of many variables and includes the role of the teacher and the nature of the course, as well as the pupils' responses.

'Before it is fully accepted . . . any new curriculum should be carefully evaluated against the ultimate criterion – its long-term effect on the children who study it . . . . The collection of test scores and other statistics is not evaluation but only the first step towards it. Evaluation is not complete until someone has made the value judgements which are based upon empirical data but which interpret the evidence and draw conclusions from it in relation to a clearly stated philosophy of the proper goals of education.'[1]

It is, perhaps, a reversal of the usual form to test the value of a course by the students' progress in it, rather than the other way around. It is quite logical though.

Public attitudes to the variety and obscurity of much of modern art have led to a belief that this is a particularly difficult school subject to assess. 'After all', it is said, 'it's all a matter of taste.' In point of fact it is not particularly difficult to assess even large amounts of art work. The usual method is for one or more experienced persons to move the works about physically until they are arranged in rank order; when this is established it may be translated into whatever formulae the school organisation required – percentage, letter-grade, form order, or whatever. It works very well and, when external moderators are used to check results, as in CSE, there is normally a high degree of unanimity between their opinions and those of the teachers. Numerative systems (so many marks for concept, colour, composition, etc) rarely work as well as holistic ones. I am not convinced that this kind of fine tuning is possible anyway. The CSE method which divides candidates' work into five describable grades is about as precise as one might sensibly expect. Is it possible to imagine giving someone 71½ per cent for art?

[1] Paul Woodring, introduction to *New Curricula*, ed. by R. W. Heath (Harper & Row, 1964).

It needs to be said that judging a single, one-off, set-piece of art work is not evaluation either, and that CSE boards are well aware of the fact. They ask teachers, examiners and moderators to look at a series of works to determine development and progress. In taking this line they are, in effect, responding to Paul Woodring's dictum that evaluation must relate to 'a clearly stated philosophy of the proper goals' and their philosophy is expressed in the Schools Council publication *Children's Growth through Creative Experience*:

'Art education is concerned with the creative growth of the child and it follows from this that progress is made when the child widens his experience. Children's work cannot therefore be usefully assessed over a short period and progress should be looked for over a term or year, rather than from month to month. The growth of technical skills is only one criterion. Progress also becomes apparent as the child acquires increasing sensitivity to pattern and colour, an awareness about the way in which forms and mechanism operate, and a growing capacity to evolve images which combine personal meaning with a power to affect others.'

This statement pre-supposes two things. Firstly, what is to be measured is development and change, not a static situation at a given moment. This I take to be a valuable concept which is applicable to any kind of personal or expressive activity. Secondly, the last sentence assumes particular objectives for art teaching, those embodied in the ideas of the expressive or appreciation rationales, and might need to be modified for assessing basic-design work. But the general principles of individual assessment can hardly be better expressed than in this statement, which follows shortly after:

'We believe . . . that a child's work can and should be criticised and assessed, taking into account *the child himself and what he is capable of.* Sincerity is an essential criterion; the work should be a genuinely personal statement or experiment. The teacher should then look for the quality of the child's reponse to the imaginative situation or problem, and for the degree of involvement. Thirdly, and particularly with older children, the teacher may assess the way materials and tools have been used, the approach to the problem and the kind of technical or inventive solution that has been found.'

It has to be assumed, of course, that the experienced teacher will not know what is to be expected from children within specific age groups and will be able to distinguish what is natural or exceptional in their work.

Having arrived at his assessment, the teacher will look for the best method of recording his conclusions. American schools have evolved much more complex forms of doing this than is yet common in Britain. The adoption of a special report form for each subject, for example, gives the teacher some opportunity of standardising his findings. The student evaluation grid shown in Figure 6, which appears in Elliot W. Eisner's *Educating Artistic Vision,* is worthy of consideration both for internal and external use. Note the tripartite comparison of each student's results with 'standard', with his group and, particularly important, with his own expected level of achievement.

	Student with Standard	Student with Group	Student with Self
Productive			
Critical			
Cultural			

Figure 6 *Student evaluation grid*

Less useful as it stands, I think, is the Student Progress Report (Figure 7) used, I believe in Minnesota schools. I would dearly like to see the 'copies of the standard' which may be obtained from the school and would shrink in horror at the thought of compiling such a thing. But the form is sound enough, even if the headings need to be adapted to fit specific curricula.

There is almost no authority on the subject of art education who does not stress the ultimate importance of pupils' self-evaluation, especially for older children. Any teacher who has instilled the confidence and knowledge of criteria into the pupils so that they can look at their own (and others) work with clear and critical eyes has completed almost the whole of his teaching task. It is never easy. Every art teacher I know can tell of his disappointment when a child heedlessly screws up good completed work or mutters 'It's all right'

STUDENT PROGRESS REPORT

Name .... Subject ....

Teacher .... Evaluation Period Ending ....

The objectives of art education in this community are based on recognized developmental norms and the recommendations of experts in art education. The estimates of achievement reported here are based upon that standard. Copies of the standard may be obtained from the school that your child is attending.

	Below Standard	Standard	Exceeds Standard
KNOWLEDGE OF:			
Content and subject matter (life)			
Procedures			
Composition			
Art History			
Aesthetics			
ATTITUDES:			
Self-confidence in art			
Interest in art			
Willingness to work hard			
Tolerance of style in art			
SKILL:			
The ability to handle materials efficiently			

Comments:

540
ART
EDUCATION

Figure 7

when asked his own opinion of a juvenile masterpiece he has slaved over. Dare I ask British teachers to try out some varient of Eisner's self-evaluation form (Figure 8) on their classes? I have not had the courage to do so – yet.

There is one important aspect of evaluation which I mentioned at the beginning of this chapter. In making judgement about the progress of our classes, all of us are implicitly commenting on our own performances. I remember once, as a form tutor many years ago,

NAME ____________________________

DATE ____________________________

NAME OF PROJECT ____________________________

DATE COMPLETED ____________________________

1. I thought this project was: Boring ____ ____ ____ ____ ____ Exciting
2. I found the work on it: Easy ____ ____ ____ ____ ____ Difficult
3. I think I learned: from this project A lot ____ ____ ____ ____ ____ A little
4. This project was my: Worst piece of work ____ ____ ____ ____ ____ Best piece of work
5. The most important things I got out of this project were: ________________

Figure 8 *Student self-evaluation form*

studying the reports of my class and finding that over two-thirds of them contained against the heading of geography some such comment as 'X must improve his/her knowledge of map work'. I am sure I was getting more information about the teacher than I was about the individual children. Either he sets his standards too high or he was not teaching this aspect of his subject as well as he would have liked. I am not sure I ever convinced him of this.

We need to evaluate the behaviour, attitude, aptitudes and products of our pupils so that we can learn how to deal with them better, and also so that we can report on their development fairly to other interested parties – particularly their parents. But we learn most about our own effectiveness by a careful study of the progress of a group. This may not be too difficult in subjects which aim to inculcate knowledge or impart specific skills – either the majority of the pupils have learned the facts and can use the skills or they cannot. Art progress is not so easily defined. There are, after all, developmental stages through which the majority of children pass, almost independent of any kind of teaching. It is not appropriate for a teacher to give himself credit for the fact that most members of his group have acquired the skill to depict overlapping forms in space or to indicate recession by a reduction in the size of objects when this perception comes naturally at a certain stage of maturation. Nor should he take too much reflected glory from the fact that he has a number of naturally gifted children in his class. There are pitfalls, but honest and precise evaluation is one of the keys to success in all education; in art it deserves more attention than it has often received.

I am sure that the time has come when the reader will wish to challenge me on the criteria which I believe should be used to judge progress in art. To paraphrase Professor Joad's famous dictum, 'It all depends on what you mean by progress . . . it all depends on what you mean by art.' One sets oneself objectives and looks to see how far they are being attained. As for my own objectives, I can only refer you back to Chapter 2, in which I tried to describe what might be meant by an 'artistically educated person'. I hope we are trying to increase the number of such persons.

I suggested that such a person:

(i) should have come to believe that art is important to himself, the community and its evolving culture;
(ii) could see a work of art as a thing in itself, rather than the expression of something else;
(iii) should realise the difference in intention and evaluation between art and craft;
(iv) would recognise that art has standards which can, to a certain extent, be objectivised?
(v) ought to be judged less on his ability to produce art than on his capacity to appreciate its values;
(vi) and should have developed his feelings of empathy, appreciation and involvement with the world.

Modern, rational curriculum planners would not even accept these as objectives at all. These, they demand, must always be capable of measurement in behaviourist terms. But how could a boy show by his behaviour alone that he believed art to be important. He could, of course, bring art books to school to show to Sir. He might choose to spend his time in the fine-art section of the school library. But this might only mean that he likes to please his teacher or that he enjoys the licensed pleasure of studying uncensored nudes. We are concerned with what a child thinks and feels – this is not always demonstrated by what he does. Is it possible to understand each child in a class and evaluate just how far he has gone along the road to genuine self-realisation through art? Probably not, though I am convinced that of all the members of the school staff the art teacher can be in the position of getting close enough to decipher the inner clues. In the last resort this is almost all that matters. The student can have the largely inborn skill-components of the subject measured in GCE and further education if this matters to him. For most people the appreciation and understanding of values are the main functions of a balanced liberal curriculum, and to this the arts subjects have a great deal to contribute. It is these factors which need to be evaluated above all.

An End and a Beginning

When I started this book I planned to conclude it with some sort of statement of my own views on the true aims of art teaching and offer some prescriptions by which these ends might be achieved. I was not absolutely sure what these would be, but after more than 30,000 words on a subject I have been teaching for nearly thirty years surely all would become clear – if only to myself? Yet I am not so very much wiser.

It is tempting for any teacher to believe that there is a right way to do his particular job. He may believe that he is already practising it; it is much more likely that he will know that he is not but that with time, experience, freedom, a lot of thinking and, perhaps, some expert guidance, he will find the key. If I have learned anything and tried to explain it in this book it is that there is not *a* key but very many. This is particularly true of the teaching – learning process in the arts. A drama, poetry, music or painting lesson contains within it an almost infinite number of separate conversations – between teacher and class, teacher and individual pupils, pupils with teacher and with each other. No prescriptive formula could encompass all the possibilities.

The book will, I hope, help some teachers (and potential teachers) to clarify their own minds about the nature of their professional task and, having done so, to be better able to communicate these concepts and purposes to their seniors and colleagues. This is important if art is going to achieve its proper place in the central core of the educational curriculum.

If all teaching is an art, and it is so very often said that it is, how much more is art teaching an art? By its very definition a work of art is not an end, it is a way and one which each person has to find for himself. This applies to the teaching process too. It is the art teacher's privileged function to preside over (and share in) the step-by-step development of each individual child's progress; to note (without too much ineffectual regret the loss of the 'innocent eye' of childhood, with all its power to charm and disarm, and the growth towards that sophisticated synthesis of experience which art can offer to the adolescent or adult.

Perhaps one can argue and rationalise too much and, in doing so, never convey a picture of the intense and personal struggle into expressive maturity which may be experienced through art.

Keith Gentle, himself a senior art inspector, has tried to recapture such feelings in this poem. I am grateful for his permission to reproduce it here.

From Where Do We Begin

When I was a child
I could easily see and feel things
They were so real, they were at the dawn of my knowing:
My experience of them was all part of my becoming.
The smell of grass when you'd finished rolling down a bank
Or the mowings through which you tumbled your hands,
Until it became a throwing game.
I hadn't thought of drawing grass,
It just was.

Later,
With my friends,
We chased through woods and trees
In the yellow evenings when the trees were black.
Our games were serious and of real intent,
And our value marked in each other's eyes
Whatever talent we could show.
For I could draw
They said.

One day back home,
A man called, a friend of the family,
'When you can play "The Bluebells of Scotland" I'll give
you a pound.'
So, there were things worth striving for,
Real achievements that grown-ups recognised,
And then there was the first box of oils
And the underground sea from 'Journey to the Centre of
the Earth'.
It recreated something for me;
They liked it.

Next
Came a lake and a glen;
My father's pound for that.
But the oils still worked in nasty lines
Even the sky wasn't as flat as it should be.
He's good at Art they said, and so
To Art School I was sent.
That's where the journey into me
Began.

It seemed,
From what they said,
That there were ways of doing things.
But I liked lights and shades across woods and fields,
And to escape into symphonies and the elemental forces.
Even so I did not exist in my imagery
Nor yet in theirs, they made that clear.
My approach was wrong
And my darks a fake.

So it was
That inside me
Nothing connected any better
For all the compromises I had made.
Any vision was passed through the jaws of discussion
And masticated on endless thoughts
The forms and images which grew in paint
Did not connect
With feeling.

But sometimes
I feel real inside
And my imagination strives for form.
Ideas grate over a sea of shallow clichés
That anchor the spirit in empty shapes. Their shapes?
Sensation breaks on a barren shore and like a blind bat
The vision flits about my bone cave
Seeking sanctuary
In real form.

From where do we begin?
That which is outside forgets;
That which is inside knows.
Of course we must learn more about the outside
Its structures, harmonies, language and order;
And how to communicate and solve problems.
Perhaps the forty minute periods repeated often
Enable us to grasp patterns and strategies
Through a certain imprinting.

Yet time flows through me
And I sense another pattern,
A more enduring and persistent reality,
Not dissolved in the acid tests of a designed solution,
But a reality that identifies meanings
Enabling me to seek their origin
And restore the language whose inner light
And outward form
Are one reality.

Above all else
The trust we seek
Was there at the beginning.
Believing that there is an inner life of images,
Rooted in sensations which we only later know,
Striving for persistence in material form,
Its times and rhythms beyond our knowing.
But yet a task more real to see
Because it's there in you and me.

Such potent yeasts are the raw material of the art teacher's craft. If we remember that, all the strategies, rationales and sequential arguments in this book fall into their rightful place.

Suggestions for Further Reading

PROLOGUE

McLuhan, Marshall, in G. E. Stearns (ed.), *McLuhan Hot and Cool* (Penguin, 1968).

THE HISTORY OF ART EDUCATION (CHAPTER 3)

MacDonald, Stuart, *The History and Philosophy of Art Education* (University of London Press, 1970).
Read, Herbert, *Education through Art* (Faber, 1964).
Sutton, Gordon, *Artisan or Artist?* (Pergamon, 1967). A history of the teaching of art and crafts in English schools.

POSSIBLE OBJECTIVES (CHAPTER 4 AND ELSEWHERE)

Field, Dick, *Change in Art Education* (Routledge & Kegan Paul, 1970).
Stockl, Meira, 'Art Integrated? The place of art in the curriculum', *Athene* (June 1974). This is published twice-yearly by the Society for Education through Art, situated at the Bath Academy of Art, Corsham.

ART AS EXPRESSION (CHAPTER 5)

Eisner, Elliott W., *Educating Artistic Vision* (Collier Macmillan, 1972). This US publication is quoted elsewhere in this book, particularly in Chapter 12, 'Evaluation'.
Witkin, Robert W., *The Intelligence of Feeling* (Heinemann, 1975). Witkin worked very closely with Malcolm Ross in the Schools Council 'Arts and the Adolescent Project', based on the University of Exeter Institute of Education (1968-72). This book, a powerful, well-researched and original defence of the subject as it is concerned with the expression of feeling, is one of the results of this work.

THE FINE-ART STRATEGY (CHAPTER 6)

Piper, D. W. (ed.), *Readings in Art and Design (After Hornsey)* (Davis Poynter, 1973).

THROUGH CRAFT TO ART (CHAPTER 7)

Open University, *The Balby Street Kids* (Open University, 1976).

Extract from radio programme no. 5 of the Open University course 'Curriculum design and development E203'.

Rasmusen, H. and Grant, A., *Sculpture from Junk* (Van Nostrand, 1967).

Rottger, Ernst, *Creative Wood Craft* (Batsford, 1961).

Rottger, Ernst, *Creative Paper Craft* (Batsford, 1973).

Rottger, Ernst and Klante, Dieter, *Surfaces in Creative Design* (Batsford, 1970).

Tomlinson, R. R., and Mills, J. F., *The Growth of Child Art* (University of London Press, 1956). This contains many examples of children's art work which appeared in the 1960 National Exhibition of Child Art. A long introduction contains contributions by Herbert Read, R. R. Tomlinson, Andrew Nairn, Eduardo Paolozzi, Victor Pasmore and others.

DESIGN FOR CONSUMERS (CHAPTER 8)

Rowland, Kurt, 'Looking and Seeing' (Ginn, 1965).

1. *Pattern and Shape*
2. *The Development of Shape*
3. *The Shapes We Need*
4. *The Shape of Towns*

Schools Council, 'Design Education 11-16' (unpublished). Introductory papers for development project 'Design in General Education', September 1976-.

BASIC DESIGN (CHAPTER 9)

Aylward, B., *Design Education in Schools* (Evans, 1973).

de Sausmarez, Maurice, *Basic Design: The Dynamics of Visual Form* (Studio Vista, 1964).

Green, Peter, *Design Education – Problem-Solving and Visual Experience* (Batsford, 1974).

Schools Council Project Team: *Design for Today* (Edward Arnold, 1976); *Looking at Design* (Edward Arnold, 1976); *Materials and Design* (Edward Arnold, 1976); *You Are a Designer* (Edward Arnold, 1976).

TEACHERS OF ART (CHAPTER 11)

Ross, Malcolm, *Arts and the Adolescent* (Evans/Methuen Educational, 1975). Schools Council Working Paper no. 54. A curriculum study from the Schools Council's 'Arts and the Adolescent Project' based at the University of Exeter Institute of Education. See *The Intelligence of Feeling* by Robert Witkin under 'Possible Objectives' above.

EVALUATION (CHAPTER 12)

Eisner, Elliott W., *Educating Artistic Vision* (Collier Macmillan, 1972). See under 'Art as Expression' above.

Lansing, Kenneth M., *Art, Artists and Art Education* (McGraw-Hill, 1969).

Richmond, W. Kenneth, *The School Curriculum* (Methuen, 1971).

Schools Council, *Children's Growth through Creative Experience – Art and Craft 8-13* (Van Nostrand, 1974).

OFFICIAL REPORTS

Board of Education, *The Education of the Adolescent* (Hadow Report) (HMSO, 1926).

Board of Education, *Secondary Education, with Special Reference to Grammar Schools and Technical High Schools* (Spens Report) (HMSO, 1938).

Board of Education, *Report on Curriculum and Examinations in Secondary Schools* (Norwood Report) (HMSO, 1941).

Department of Education, *Art in Schools,* Department of Education Survey no. 11 (HMSO, 1946).

Ministry of Education, *Art Education*, Ministry of Education pamphlet no. 6 (HMSO, 1946).

Ministry of Education, *Half Our Future* (Newsom Report) (HMSO, 1963).

National Union of Teachers, *The Curriculum of the Secondary School* (NUT, 1952).

GENERAL

Colour Review, the art teachers' journal, published by Winsor & Newton, Wealdstone, Harrow, Middlesex, and sent free to all art-teachers.

Selection of papers from the Association of Art Advisers, developed from the work of the 1974 Conference of the Association on the function of art education in secondary schools. Contributors: Keith Gentle, Ernest Goodman, David Aspin, Maurice Barrett, Norman Birch, Bob Clement, Neil White. These papers are available from most county art advisers and inspectors.